Art as Extraordinary Science
A paradigm for the 21st Century

Jenny Waller

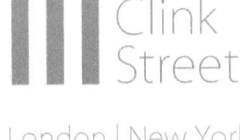

London | New York

Published by Clink Street Publishing 2016

Copyright © 2016

First edition.

The author asserts the moral right under the Copyright, Designs and Patents Act 1988 to be identified as the author of this work.

All rights reserved. No part of this publication may be reproduced, stored in a retrieval system or transmitted, in any form or by any means without the prior consent of the author, nor be otherwise circulated in any form of binding or cover other than that with which it is published and without a similar condition being imposed on the subsequent purchaser.

ISBN: PB 9781911110088
EB 9781911110095

Contents

Introduction 5

Part 1: Theory

1: The problem of explanation 11
1.1 Stephan Körner and the horse beside the writing desk 11
1.2 Two case studies 13

2: The characteristics of paradigms 20
2.1 Invisibility 21
2.2 Incommensurability 22
2.3 Permeability 23
2.4 Potency 23
2.5 Metaphors for paradigms 25

3: Researching paradigms 27
3.1 Soft Systems Methodology (SSM) 27
3.2 Multi-dimensional grids 30
3.3 Metaphor 31

4: The Framework of Educational Assumptions 33
4.1 Normal Science 35
4.2 Professional Practice 41
4.3 Extraordinary Science 44
4.4 Voodoo 51
4.5 The dynamics of the Framework 55

Part 2: The historical perspective

5: The historical narrative 61
5.1 The medieval workshop 62
5.2 The Renaissance academy 65
5.3 The formal classroom 67
5.4 The masterclass 71
5.5 The modernist studio 74

6: Interpreting the historical narrative 77
6.1 Traditional interpretations 77
6.2 Problems with traditional interpretations 77

6.3 The paradoxes of Fine Art education 78
6.4 The historical narrative and the Framework of Educational Assumptions 86

7: Art and the university 89
7.1 The problem of integration 90
7.2 Art as a discipline 91
7.3 The Hornsey revolution 93
7.4 Analysing Fine Art 94
7.5 Experimental paradigms 95
7.6 Experimental paradigms and the Framework of Educational Assumptions 98
7.7 Who's influencing whom? 100

Part 3: Fieldwork

8: The role of discourse analysis 105
8.1 Foucault and the theory of discourse analysis 105
8.2 Discourse analysis in practice 112
8.3 Educational discourse 115

9: The research 117
9.1 Data gathering 117
9.2 The structural analysis 121
9.3 The thematic analysis 124

10: Structural analysis findings 125
10.1 Dominance analysis 125
10.2 Exchange ratio analysis 126
10.3 Exchange analysis 127
10.4 Interaction analysis 134
10.5 Structural analysis and the Framework of Educational Assumptions 135

11: Thematic analysis findings 138
11.1 Identifying the themes 138
11.2 Theme descriptions 138
11.3 The distribution of the themes 155
11.4 Thematic analysis and the Framework of Educational Assumptions 158

12: Art as Extraordinary Science 163
12.1 A 21st century paradigm 163
12.2 Teaching Extraordinary Science 165
12.3 Case study: Steve Jobs 166

References 171

Introduction

'…art education is radically undertheorized.'[1]

Ever since Fine Art moved into the universities in the 1970's, the pressure has been on to find answers not only to tricky questions about the academic status of Fine Art, but also to what art historian Carl Goldstein calls its fundamental and enduring problematic – whether art can be taught at all.

> The single question that has haunted the history of art teaching from the renaissance to the twentieth Century…precisely what should be taught and whether the essence of art can be taught, or can *art* be taught? (Goldstein, 1996, pp. 4-5)

Fast forward to the twenty-first century and these answers seem further away than ever. The very title of art educationalist James Elkins' *Why Art Cannot be Taught* (2001) signals that both the phrase and the concept are still part of the mainstream discourse of art education. According to Elkins (2001), our current model of Fine Art teaching does not even have a name. His only suggestion is "post-war Art Schools" which would signify a commitment to "non-aesthetic forms of art" (Elkins, 2008, p. 2). There is no curriculum in art departments, with art programmes "marked by an absence of almost all restrictions on the kind of courses that can be taught" (Elkins, 2001, p. 38). The underlying order of the field itself has been lost, since "contemporary artists and critics don't care very much what is counted as art and what isn't, and they are likely to accept anything (billboards, miniature golf) as a visual art" (p. 50). Art students themselves are mediocre, "average and uninventive" (p. 68), and traditional skills have been neglected in favour of the seduction of the "giddy growth in new media" (p. 75). Art schools are an illusion. It may look as if art is being taught in all sorts of ways but "what is done in studio classrooms is often the determined opposite of the customs and habits of the older academies or else the lingering, nearly inaudible echo of the Bauhaus" (p. 39). In contrast to the certainties of the past, art departments are experiencing an abrupt disconnect with the past and facing a future that is both unnameable and impossible to explain.

---

1   Elkins, 2008, p. 1

For art curator Charles Esche, Fine Art remains a subject that is "by many standards unteachable and unlearnable" (Esche, 2009, p. 102). Similarly Daniel Birnbaum (I) reflects in his dialogical encounter with Adorno/the devil (He).

I: Well, art is taught. But nobody seems to know how.

He: And yet people like you keep doing it for years. Isn't that hypocritical, even cynical?

I: 'I don't think art can be taught. I really don't,' says John Baldessari …which seems a bit paradoxical perhaps. I don't think one could call John a cynic…he has been teaching art, whatever that may mean, for half a century, so his account is probably realistic…

He: …so perhaps we should end the conversation here.
(Birnbaum, 2009, p. 232)

This isn't just an abstract philosophical problem either. It can be tough for art tutors to deal with the accountabilities of the university system without some sort of straightforward explanation at hand. As tutor Louisa Buck wistfully reflects, "How do you teach something that has no parameters? No subject, no medium, no process, no professional protocol?" (Tickner, 2008, p. 93).

This then is the challenge before us: to find a way of explaining Fine Art in the context of the university.

Part 1: Theory looks at the theory of explanation, and culminates in a framework to use as an analytical tool. This is the Framework of Educational Assumptions, described in detail in Chapter 4, which gives us the quadrants of Normal Science, Professional Practice, Extraordinary Science and Voodoo.

Part 2: The historical perspective looks at the history of Fine Art education in relation to the Framework.

Finally, *Part 3: Fieldwork* presents the findings of research carried out with a Fine Art studio group as part of my PhD thesis (Waller, 2014). Using discourse analysis, the research provides insight into contemporary Fine Art teaching with a view to understanding where we are now, and how the 21st Century paradigm of Fine Art in the university can be described as Extraordinary Science.

And interestingly, this conclusion may turn out to just as interesting for the sciences as it is for Fine Art. Back in the '70s, researchers Risenhoover and Blackburn (1976) used the analogy of new settlers arriving in territories already occupied by "old-timers" to describe the arrival of art as a new discipline. They anticipated that its impact would be significant, with art tutors teaching the university about "creativity and productivity…highly important matters regarding the creative side" (pp. 212-3). Art tutors would be better at identifying subjective criteria for excellence than their science colleagues, and at establishing the conditions for "sparking innovations" given their propensity to "try something new for the fun of it" (pp. 206-8).

Risenhoover and Blackburn expected the influencing process to happen naturally over the years through a mutually satisfactory process of contagion. Yet there's little evidence that this has happened so far. Perhaps it's only when Fine Art and the university can find a way of explaining themselves to each other that this integration can finally take place with considerable benefit to both sides.

Part 1:
Theory

1: The problem of explanation

'To a man with a hammer everything begins to look like a nail. But because we can come to know things only in terms of other things, every 'explanation', however convincing, is merely a model; a comparison of something with something else.'[2]

1.1 Stephan Körner and the horse beside the writing desk

A useful starting point for the problem of explaining Fine Art at the university is to establish what we know about explanation in the first place. For this we can turn to Stephan Körner, a philosopher in the field of logic and classification.

To illustrate the issues associated with explanation, Körner (1974) asks us to imagine the scenario of a horse appearing beside his writing desk. The event itself isn't a problem. The real problem is, how can we explain it?

According to Körner, we can explain the event "naturally" if we can find reasons for it which don't challenge our assumptions about horses and writing desks in general, and this horse and writing desk in particular. A natural explanation would be that, for example, the horse has wandered in from the field next door.

But what if there is no natural explanation? What if there is no field next to Körner's study? What if his writing desk is up the stairs on the first floor? In that case it's possible to find an explanation by going back to the event itself to reclassify it, to understand it in a different way. Maybe, for example, the horse is actually a man who for some reason has been misidentified (Körner, 1974, p. 62), since lighting can be poor, shadows may fall, and our perceptions deceive.

If this still doesn't give us an answer, we'll generally give up around now and say that the event simply can't be explained. But in philosophical terms, Körner reminds us that "unexplained" is not the same as "unexplainable".

> If...I saw a horse beside my writing desk and did not believe any of a number of propositions tracing its journey from a more likely place to my room, I should regard its appearance at my desk as unexplained, though not necessarily as unexplainable. (Körner, 1974, p. 61)

---

2 McGilchrist, 2009, p. 98

In fact we can still explain it, but only by revising our assumptions about the nature either of horses or writing desks or both (Körner, 1974, p. 61). Unfortunately Körner doesn't suggest what this kind of explanation might be, but it's safe to say it'll be surprising and challenge our day-to-day understanding of the world. Could it be a magic horse?

According to Körner's logic, there's always an explanation for everything, as long as we're prepared to revise our assumptions and engage in the metaphysical activity of creating meaning by "the exhibition of implicitly accepted categorial frameworks…their critical examination, and sometimes, also…their modification" (Körner, 1974, p. 59).

In reality, though, Körner reminds us how rarely this happens, given the strength of our instinct *not* to question our assumptions. Our commitments to what he calls our *categorial frameworks* run deep, and are "easily confused with truth" (Körner, 1974, p. 24). Indeed, logically, these frameworks are incorrigible (p. 14)[3] when viewed from the inside, ruled by their own unassailable logics: literally, their assumptions can't be questioned by the people who accept them.

But if "the propositions and distinctions which are characteristic of a categorical framework are incorrigible if viewed from the inside", they are "corrigible if viewed from the outside of it" (Körner, 1974, p. 14): "internal incorrigibility does not imply external incorrigibility" (p. 20). That's why questioning assumptions is always so risky. It may change what we think we know and challenge our certainties: we may have to change our minds.

So it's not surprising that it may be a thankless task. As Körner (1974) notes, if observations are "characteristic of one's own categorial framework, their familiarity may make them seem trivial; if of another's radically different categorial framework, their unfamiliarity may make them seem absurd" (p. 65).

Look at what happens when researcher Sarah Thornton ([2008]2009) sets out to investigate the paradigm of the artist.

> During my stay in Los Angeles, I asked all sorts of people, What is an artist? It's an irritatingly basic question, but reactions were so aggressive that I came to the conclusion that I must be violating some taboo. When I asked the students, they looked completely shocked. 'That's not fair!' said one. 'You can't ask that!' said another. An artist with a senior position in a university art department accused me of being 'stupid', and a major curator said, 'Ugh. All your questions are only answerable in a

---

3 In philosophical terms, an incorrigible proposition is one which, if honestly believed, cannot be mistaken, and is intrinsically unverifiable or unfalsifiable. According to Körner (1974, p. 25), most metaphysical propositions belong to this category.

way that is almost tautological...I mean, for me, an artist is someone who makes art.' (Thornton, [2008]2009, pp. 51-52)

Thornton's question "What is an artist?" seems innocent enough: she's looking for insight into the paradigm, not making judgements about it. But the very act of asking invokes strong defences. Just as Körner predicts, to those within the paradigm the answer is so obvious as to make the question seem not only trivial but also "stupid" (Thornton, [2008]2009, p. 51) or "tautological...an artist is someone who makes art". Thornton also notes the unexpected aggression her question produces, leading her to conclude she must be "violating some taboo" (p. 52). Indeed she is: the taboo of making assumptions explicit, since what can be made explicit can also be challenged.

> What the teacher spells out, the pupil can question. What he assumes, especially from a position of unchallenged legitimacy, his pupils will tend to swallow whole and unawares. (Hudson, [1972]1974), p. 43)

In the same way Elkins (2001) is also wary of any external perspective which invokes corrigibility: "one can also ask if it is a good idea to keep trying to make rational sense out of art teaching" (p. 189), since "...in the end, if it were possible to produce a full account of how art is taught, it might be a boring, pernicious document, something that should be locked away" (p. 191).

Meanwhile for those outside the Fine Art paradigm, its characteristics may seem simply absurd. Take for example the paradox that art cannot be taught but is taught. Art teachers accept the paradox, working "right at the centre of the contradiction" (Elkins, 2001, p. 97), but to many if not most outside the discipline the proposition seems nonsensical. As one lecturer put it to me, "it's beyond paradox...impossible". Körner seems to be right about that too.

1.2 Two case studies

The difficulties we have with finding explanations that don't present themselves naturally are illustrated in two well-known studies of Fine Art teaching: *Art students observed* (Madge & Weinberger, 1973) and the influential book we've noted earlier, Elkins' *Why art cannot be taught* (2001). Both studies look for ways to explain art at the university; it's fair to say that both fail.

1.2.1 Art students observed (Madge & Weinberger, 1973)

Madge and Weinberger's *Art students observed* (1973) is an ethnographic study of Fine Art education at the fictional Midville College[4] from 1967-69, at the time when the integration of Fine Art to the university system is just beginning. Their research is funded by the Social Science Research Council (SSRC), carried out by a team of researchers over five years, and regarded as methodologically sound. It's based "loosely…[on]…participant observation" (p. 21) and supplemented by a wealth of qualitative data from interviews and questionnaires with staff, students, and parents as well as quantitative data about student qualifications and destinations.[5]

For Brighton (1992, p. 139), Madge and Weinberger's research is "seminal to the study of art students in higher education, although this is not always acknowledged" because of the wealth of reliable data it provides: "descriptive rather than explanatory in character" (p. 140), this is pure research where the facts are allowed to speak for themselves.

At the heart of the description is the *Illustrative section* (Madge & Weinberger, 1973, pp. 123-187) which makes up 20 per cent of the book's content and consists of documentation about 14 students, including tutors' reports, autobiographical statements from the students themselves, and data from the observers' notebooks. As empirical data, this material certainly has the potential to provide insights into the paradigm of Fine Art at a particular moment in time.

In the event, however, the descriptive status of the data is compromised by Madge and Weinberger's (1973) commentary which reveals a commitment to a particular set of social and educational assumptions which are never fully examined. Consider their opening statement:

> There is little or no consensus either among artists or among their public about the nature and purpose of artistic activity. Socialization into art is therefore socialization into nobody quite knows what. (Madge & Weinberger, 1973, p. 15)

Here the unexamined assumptions are that consensus is necessary, that purpose and clarity are desirable, and that if Fine Art lacks these qualities, it is in the wrong.

---

4 Coventry Polytechnic, according to Tickner (2008).

5 Specifically, the research includes transcripts of conversations with students, photographs of student work, a standardised questionnaire for students, an agree/disagree exercise for students at Midville and other colleges for comparison, interviews with students planning to go to art school, interviews with parents of students who both do and do not intend to study Fine Art, data about student destinations, and staff reports on the students being observed.

The clues about Madge and Weinberger's assumptions are everywhere throughout the research text: for example when they contrast Fine Art students and their "extremely fluid and ill-defined rôle" with medical and law students whose roles have " a considerable degree of definition and stability" (Madge & Weinberger, 1973, p. 19), or when they compare the career prospects of art students with the "hazardous existence and ephemeral rewards of the pop group" (p. 21).

The analysis of their statement of the art student's predicament below (Table 1) reveals how these assumptions act throughout the research discourse, shaping our response to the data.

Statement	Madge and Weinberger's assumptions
The art student's predicament	Art students are in a predicament; all is not well.
He has opted out of the dominant occupational system;	It is good to be part of the dominant occupational system. Opting out is problematic.
He is driven to behave as though he had access to a charisma which may not be his to command;	Art does not have the status to justify authoritative behaviour of this kind; artists should be more humble.
and he has to justify this to himself and to his peers and teachers, in intellectualised terms and conditions of almost unbearable ambiguity.	Everyone has to justify themselves in terms of their performance. Art students struggle to be intellectuals. Ambiguity is unbearable.

Table 1. An analysis of the underlying assumptions of Madge and Weinberger's (1973) statement of the art student's predicament.

Madge and Weinberger's (1973) treatment of the theme of stability shows the limitations of this approach. As the research progresses, the authors realise that change, uncertainty, and ambiguity are something of a central theme: "our study has demonstrated the ambiguities of the process of socialization into art" (p. 27). This might well imply a fundamental affinity between "fluidity" and the artistic temperament: "societies provide such roles in order to accommodate unpredictable personalities" (p. 20).[6] Here the authors seem on the verge of insight into the central role of uncertainty in the Fine Art paradigm. In the event, however,

---

6 In support of this point Madge and Weinberger quote S. F. Nadel (1957), who cites "poets, artists [and] millionaires" as examples of society's eccentrics for whom fluidity is acceptable (Madge & Weinberger, 1973, p. 20).

they choose to dismiss it as unfortunate and problematic. The ambiguity the students experience is "almost unbearable" (p. 21); the process of disorientation in the studio is "unnerving and depressing in the extreme", especially for girls (p. 276); while for the tutors, the debate about the role of verbal analysis in studio practice needs to be resolved by "a more coherent policy" (p. 277). In fact "the whole situation [is] problematic" (p. 17) as much for the authors as for the art students they observe.

We know that problems of reflexivity and positionality are recognised in the research literature of the time (for example Garfinkel, 1967), but Madge and Weinberger (1973) seem unaware of the extent to which their assumptions about education and society colour what they observe.

In the end, Madge and Weinberger are forced to conclude that art education does not make sense to them, and that "almost everything about art education, and about art itself, remains almost totally in question" (Madge & Weinberger, 1973, p. 26). The sense of disappointment is palpable. Five years of research, all methodologically sound, seem to have led to nothing. How has this happened?

Madge and Weinberger are certainly right in concluding that Fine Art education can't be explained in any normal way, given their unreflective assumptions about educational and social values. The wealth of evidence they have gathered seems confused and contradictory, leading them to conclude that art itself is confused and contradictory.

But as we have seen, to be unexplained is not the same as to be unexplainable. Had Madge and Weinberger been explicit about their assumptions, and accepted the possibility that those of art students might be different from their own, explanations would have been possible. As educational ethnographer George Spindler warns:

> If educators assimilate ethnography and in doing so erase its identity, ethnography will not be capable of challenging educationalist assumptions and suggesting innovations in educational practice. (Spindler, 1982, p. 18)

1.2.2 Why art cannot be taught (Elkins, 2001)

The title of Elkins' book *Why art cannot be taught* signals his intention to exorcise once and for all the question identified by Goldstein as haunting Fine Art education from its beginnings (Goldstein, 1996). This is, according to Elkins, a book of two parts: "one concerns the historical and critical issues around the development of Art Schools…and the other concerns critiques" (Elkins, 2008, p. 9).

1: THE PROBLEM OF EXPLANATION

In the first part, Elkins' historical survey follows art historians Pevsner (1940) and Goldstein (1996) in tracing the development of art education from "the ancient art schools" (p. 5) to the modernist studios of the Bauhaus and beyond (p. 37). His proposal is to use teaching in its taken-for-granted sense[7] as a template to show historically where art education does or, more likely, judging by the title, does not fit the pattern. So Elkins' primary interest is in "curricula – the experiences a student might have had from year to year in various academies, workshops and art schools" (p. 5), the structure of the teaching institutions, and the quest for academic prestige which has a particularly contemporary relevance.

> It is often said that Renaissance artists rebelled against the medieval system and attempted to have their craft (which did not require a university degree) raised to the level of a profession (which would require a university degree), a status they eventually achieved by instituting art academies. (Elkins, 2001, p. 7)

Elkins produces a coherent, if selective, historical analysis, which as we saw in the *Introduction*, ends abruptly at the end of the twentieth Century without providing any insights into contemporary practice. This has happened because Elkins' focus on traditional educational themes such as curriculum or academic status has taken his attention away from what's actually happening in the art schools, events which are central to the paradigm of Fine Art education but unavailable to his analysis.

The second and significantly longer part of Elkins' text focuses on studio critiques.[8] Elkins is drawn to the glamour of critiques, describing them as "nearly inaccessible, unlit, dangerous and utterly seductive" (p. 191), but he's also frustrated by their elusiveness: "we know very little about *how* we teach and learn" (p. 1). Working "on the assumption that it is a good idea to try for some measure of clarity", since "in most subjects clarity and sense are ultimate goals…the principles of physics are best when they are clear"(p. 190), he deploys the sociological research toolbox with some enthusiasm[9], using a combination of observation, transcription, discourse analysis, personal experience, and reflection

---

7   Such is the strength of the traditional educational paradigm that Elkins feels no need to be explicit about it, any more than Madge and Weinberger (1973). Goldstein (1996) is more aware of the issue when he notes that "…these terms [school and academy] are so freighted with ideological preconceptions that to use either one of them is to conjure up an image of an organisation with a definite program, conceived with particular goals in view" (p. 5).

8   Indeed Elkins (2008) suggests that a more appropriate title for the book would be *A handbook of critiques* (p. 7).

9   Elkins sees many possibilities for new ways of thinking by applying social sciences thinking to art education (Elkins, 2001, p. 41).

in a bid to find an explanation about what goes on. Elkins even flirts with pseudo-scientific methodologies, developing a list of research questions based on "real-world hypotheses" (p. 168) to test assumptions about critiques such as subjectivity or "the developmental narrative" in an objective way, which could then be compared to statements by artists and critics themselves.[10] Elkins does emerge with some analytical insights, for example the pattern of "seduction… wooing and refusal" (p. 237) derived from an examination of critique transcripts, the classification of different types of critiques, or the "four-step chain of questions" tool (p. 175). But he's the first to admit that these insights don't take him much closer to the heart of the matter. In the end, art isn't physics and no amount of research can explain critiques which remain "the most irrational form of educational evaluation that exists in any field. I think of them as 99% irrational" (Elkins, 2008, p. 7). Elkins concludes that if Fine Art critiques can't be understood rationally, they can't be explained at all and the attempt is pointless:

> It does not make sense to understand how art is taught…I am not sure that it is ultimately such a good idea. (Elkins, 2001, p. 190)

Elkins has reached the same impasse as Madge and Weinberger (1973), and for the same reasons.

1.2.3 Conclusions

Both studies conclude that Fine Art teaching can't be explained naturally in terms of our normal assumptions about education.

> Education assumes that people learn by being taught, that it consists of a social enterprise of knowledgeable people teaching people who are less knowledgeable and typically, not surprisingly, less powerful and less well-placed. (Becker, 1990, p. 237)

The fact that neither study examines or revisits these assumptions is hardly surprising, given that the prevailing paradigm of education is unusually potent and well-defended against criticism[11] to the extent that "it is inseparable from judgements of value" (Peters, 1967, p. 2), all of them positive:

---

10 For example one research suggestion is "to explore what it means to be taken seriously as an artist. Take an artwork done by someone else, and place it among your own. See what kind of stories the critique panellists come up with in order to explain how that work is one of your own. Hypothesis: judgement is subjective and influenced by the context of the artist's work" (p. 169).

11 As Peters (1967) observes, no other social institution enjoys quite this prestige or unassailability (p. 2).

Education is like reform…it would be as much of a contradiction to say "My son has been educated but has learned nothing of value" as it would be to say "my son has been reformed but has changed in no way for the better'. (Peters, 1967, p. 4)

But if we want to find a way of explaining art teaching, we're going to have to examine some of these strongly-held assumptions. We have been warned.

2: The characteristics of paradigms

'It is the assumptions, prejudices, and implicit metaphors that are the true burden of what passes between teacher and taught.'[12]

In our discussion so far, we've seen that the idea of categorial frameworks or paradigms is central to explanation. So before we go any further, let's review what we know about paradigms and how they work.

For Thomas Kuhn in his classic text *The Structure of Scientific Revolutions* ([1962]1970), the paradigm is "the fundamental unit" (p. 11) of education, representing the "constellation of beliefs, values, techniques, and so on shared by the members of a given community" (p. 175). Kuhn's field is science with its own special characteristics, but his concept of the paradigm is widely accepted across the disciplines. As Kuhn himself points out, "historians of literature, of music, of the arts, of political development, and of many other human activities have long described their subjects in the same way" (p. 208). Across the disciplines all students study the paradigms of their field as essential preparation for membership of their chosen community, committing to a shared set of values and practices. For teachers, the responsibility of passing on the paradigms of their discipline or profession to the next generation is implicit in their membership of that community (p. 177).

If the concept of the paradigm is fundamental to education, it is nevertheless difficult to define with any precision. An early "sympathetic" reader of Kuhn points out that "the term is used in at least twenty-two ways" in his text (Kuhn, [1962]1970, p. 181), prompting him to consider, briefly, more specific alternative terms for some usages[13]. But if Kuhn's account falls short of a precise definition, it is nevertheless clear about the defining characteristics of paradigms.

---

12 Hudson, [1972]1974, p. 43

13 For example, *disciplinary matrix* or *symbolic generalisations*. *Theory* is ruled out as too restrictive (p.182). Not surprisingly, this research encounters similar issues with the plasticity of the term. With Kuhn, however, we take the view that this is a strength rather than a weakness.

2: THE CHARACTERISTICS OF PARADIGMS

2.1 Invisibility

Perhaps the most defining and also frustrating characteristic of paradigms is that they are invisible. Paradigms represent ways of seeing and thinking about the world which, to those who commit to them, are so self-evident as to need no explanation: "scientists do not see something as something else; instead, they simply see it" (Kuhn [1962]1970), p. 85). For information scientists Bowker and Star (2000) there is considerable irony in the fact that the paradigms that most affect us are also the least recognised:

> Remarkably for such a central part in our lives, we stand for the most part in formal ignorance of the social and moral order created by these invisible, potent entities. (Bowker & Star, 2000, p. 3)

Indeed, "the easier they are to use, the harder they are to see" (p. 33). This is the phenomenon noted by Elkins (2001, p. 1) when he observes the tendency of art tutors to see "what happens in art classes...as timeless and natural" and incapable of change.

Although education is certainly identified with a visible paraphernalia of curricula, "textbooks, lectures and...exercises" (Kuhn [1962]1970, p. 43), for Kuhn these are no more than "abstractions" from the wider sets of values and beliefs which make up the paradigm. So paradigms may include rules, but are not defined by them, since they can be transmitted without any explicit rules at all: "rules, I suggest, derive from paradigms, but paradigms can guide research even in the absence of rules" (p. 42). From this perspective, educating students in a particular discipline is less about teaching facts than about showing students how to see and understand the facts that are important to them. In this way paradigms are "more binding and more complete" (p. 46) than any explicit set of rules could be.

For students of particular disciplines, the invisible, taken-for-granted nature of paradigms has obvious functional advantages, since it means they can work within their chosen field without wasting time attempting to redefine or defend the "hypothetical rules of the game" (Kuhn, [1962]1970, p. 47).

But it does make research into paradigms something of a challenge. It's no good asking people directly since in all probability they will be "little better than laymen at characterizing the bases of their field, its legitimate problems and methods" (Kuhn, [1962]1970, p. 47). Instead, "we must look for indirect and behavioural evidence" (p. 115).[14] As Elkins (2001) reflects:

> In practice, it is not usually a good idea to press teachers for assumptions…they are usually aware of their reasons, but they often don't know much about the assumptions that are behind the reasons. (Elkins, 2001, p. 177)

2.2 Incommensurability

Another difficulty with paradigms is that they are not generally *commensurable*, that is, based on common assumptions that make it easy for us to fit them together or make direct comparisons between them. Borrowing Wittgenstein's metaphor, Kuhn describes paradigms as members of "natural families, each constituted by a network of overlapping and crisscross resemblances"(Kuhn, [1962]1970, p. 45). And just as with family members, relationships may be more or less harmonious.

In fact as families go, paradigms tend to be notoriously inharmonious. Kuhn's research suggests that it's rare for two paradigms to coexist peacefully in the same intellectual space (Kuhn, [1962]1970, p. ix). He uses visual Gestalt as an example of the problem. When people are shown images that can be seen in different ways, and "the marks on paper that were first seen as a bird are now seen as an antelope, or vice versa" (p. 85), they can see only one image at a time. One way of seeing is at the expense of the other. In the same way, different disciplines provide different pictures from the same data. As Körner (1970) points out, "psychology, anthropology and comparative linguistics bear witness to the variety of ways in which different persons and groups of persons differentiate the world or experience" (p. 2).

Unlike Gestalt subjects, however, academics can't simply switch views whenever they want. Belonging to a discipline means committing to one paradigm or another. As a result, "schools guided by different paradigms are always slightly at cross-purposes" (Kuhn, [1962]1970, p. 112), leading to arguments where both sides "are bound partly to talk through each other" (p. 148). Given that paradigms are also invisible, it's not surprising that the reasons behind such conflicts often go unrecognised and, in the absence of the "enlightened common sense" recommended by Körner as the best adjudicator in such cases (1970, p. 12), remain unresolved.

---

14 This observation is in contrast to the preference of social science research for eliciting information directly through questionnaires.

2.3 Permeability

Although paradigms seem permanent and secure to those who share them, in reality they are permeable and subject to change over time. As our knowledge of the world changes, so does the way we see it. Kuhn devotes much of *The Structure of Scientific Revolutions* to investigating how and why such changes take place, adopting as a central tenet the historical observation that "scientific communities have again and again been converted to new paradigms" (Kuhn, [1962]1970, p. 152). At any given time, a particular paradigm has the potential to be different from what comes before or after it, and is open to the influence of wider social and cultural change. According to Bowker and Star (2000), it is often only at the point of change, when the structure of the paradigm is breaking down, that its existence is actually revealed for the first time (p. 35).

The permeability of paradigms can give rise to considerable tension as people who are committed to a particular version of paradigm simply can't change. For this reason new paradigms tend to coincide with new generations of thinkers. As Max Planck "sadly remarked… 'a new scientific truth does not triumph by convincing its opponents and making them see the light, but rather because its opponents eventually die, and a new generation grows up that is familiar with it.' " (Kuhn, [1962]1970, p. 151).

2.4 Potency

An illustration of the potency of paradigms is provided by psychologist Liam Hudson in *The cult of the fact* ([1972]1974). Hudson describes his book as an autobiographical "dig… into the intellectual training" (p. 29) he receives at Oxford in the 1950's and gives us his personal account of the process of committing to, and subsequently living with, the paradigms of one's profession.[15] The context of Hudson's account is the intellectual crisis he faces at the height of his career as an academic psychologist when he realises that he not only no longer believes in the empiricist ideals of research to which he has committed throughout his career, but has little insight into how or why he came to believe them in the first place. The trigger for this realisation is reading the German poet Rilke's sonnet about a girl and a unicorn and realising that the mythical unicorn, which has no conceivable empirical status, nevertheless constitutes a more powerful psychological insight than anything produced by the "thousands now practising psychological research" (p. 28). In Bowker and Star's (2000) terms,

---
15 Hudson of course is no more an artist than Kuhn, but we can take his insights as equally universal.

Hudson's crisis represents the point of breakdown where the paradigms he has unconsciously adopted start to become visible.

Hudson's attempts to rethink the terms of his "indoctrination" (Hudson, [1972]1974, p. 98) prove surprisingly difficult, however. Where did his assumptions come from? Not from the lectures and set texts provided by the university, since the young Hudson has paid little attention to them, attending few lectures and reading even fewer texts.

> I read articles, and skipped to and fro in longer works, but in two years read not a single book of philosophy from cover to cover… in a curious sense… what we did lacked content. It was an activity; something one did – like swimming or playing the piano. (Hudson, [1972]1974, p. 37).

The real teaching takes place in small group seminars with a series of "friendly, formidable lecturers" who he describes as "the managers of our reality" (Hudson, [1972]1974, p. 41). Hudson unquestioningly absorbs the principles he comes to recognise later as a kind of "Anglo-Saxon empiricism" (p. 41) characterised by "the concern for logic, the avoidance of feeling, the ideal of clarity, hostility to metaphysics…" (p. 35). Hudson's tutors have total intellectual control over their students to the extent of deciding "what was worth discussing and what was not" (p. 41), or who to reference and who to ignore: "whole areas of thought, contemporary and historical, were tacitly rejected as illegitimate, unacceptable, bad" (p. 98). Even as a postgraduate, Hudson remembers that:

> Assumptions about research were rarely discussed, and as far as I can recall, never critically examined. Sustaining them, inarticulate, were more pervasive beliefs about knowledge itself. (Hudson, [1972]1974, p. 41)

As he is indoctrinated into the values and beliefs of the empirical tradition, Hudson's intellectual landscape quickly polarises into "the most elementary categories of which man is capable: us and them, clean and dirty, right and wrong" (Hudson, [1972]1974, p. 97). This polarisation is efficiently reinforced by the politics of the university system, whereby "students who wish to question the prevailing orthodoxy tend in practice to receive poor degrees" (p. 101). This goes deeper than politics, however. In a demonstration of the incommensurability of paradigms, Hudson reflects on how learning to see the world in one way leaves him forever unable to see alternatives: "as a student, I could not understand Sartre…nor can I now, except by the most strenuous effort" (p. 97).

In the end, Hudson's intellectual crisis is a result of paradigm change. As the field of psychology develops over time, earlier assumptions come to seem flawed and barely credible. For example, speaking of the exclusion of context by the early psychologists, Hudson can only acknowledge that "an oversight of such magnitude is now a little hard to credit" (Hudson, [1972]1974, p. 38) and that, in retrospect, "most of the material we learnt is now outmoded. Its range was in any case narrow, at times eccentrically so" (p. 41). As he learns at some personal cost, "academic orthodoxies do live long and stubborn lives; but they eventually collapse, frequently with surprising speed" (p. 103). Hudson's encounter with Rilke's unicorn has its own wistful significance in this context, as a symbol of an intellectual trajectory which could have been his. Ultimately, though, his commitments will have to stand, in spite of his reservations: "what we did, we did thoroughly" (p. 42).

Hudson's account provides a testimony to the potency of paradigms as a kind of indoctrination. Once we acquire them, paradigms are for life, and Hudson's attempts to reconstruct his own intellectual history meet with limited success. "Even with the benefit if hindsight", he confesses, "I can still detect only chinks in the armour of those who taught us" (Hudson, [1972]1974, p. 98). Hudson accepts the need for intellectual training and its corresponding restrictions, since " a teacher who leaves his students' minds open…is scarcely a teacher at all" (p. 98). He's loyal to his Oxford education for its "sense of excitement and spiritual energy" (p. 99). Yet when he characterises students of a particular ideology as "victims" (p. 98), or pleads for "elbow room" (p. 99), he evoke the darker, more repressive side of this potency. It would be hard to read Hudson as ultimately at peace with his intellectual world.

2.5 Metaphors for paradigms

According to linguists George Lakoff and Mark Johnson ([1980]2003), metaphor informs most of our conceptual systems (p. 4), while for Andrew Ortony, understanding these underlying metaphors will help us either to interpret systems more accurately or gain new insights (Ortony, [1979]1998, p. 5). So it's useful to conclude our discussion of the characteristics of paradigms by looking at the metaphors used to describe them.

Kuhn's ([1962]1970) recurring metaphor is of the paradigm as a mapping tool. In a world which "is too complex and varied to be explored at random" (p. 109), paradigms are tools for grouping together "different bundles of experience" (p. 135), helping us to review both where we are and where we might go (p. 121). This mapping process is comprehensive, working down from the "experience of the race, the culture" to "finally, the profession"

(p. 140), and includes metaphysical belief (p. 184) as well as experience. The metaphor of the mapping tool suggests that paradigms are a positive and purposeful way of managing the world.

However Kuhn's famous metaphor of paradigm change as revolution is in stark contrast to the image of the peaceful map-maker. The violence of the metaphor adds a whole new dimension to this otherwise rational process.

Bowker and Star (2000) also use an exploratory metaphor for paradigms. For them, the vast information space of all possible knowledge is a forest, within which trees and bushes represent different classification structures. The challenge is to define the forest in the most appropriate way: "you may write a basic manual of forestry, or paint a landscape, compose an opera, or improve the maps used throughout." Their metaphor is more complex that Kuhn's, however, since in the darkness of the forest, the power of paradigms is limited and intractable areas remain which are, through accident or design, "left wild, or in darkness, or even unmapped (that is, some ambiguity will remain)" (p. 32).

Finally, Hudson ([1972]1974) describes our cultural and intellectual life as a river where paradigms, at the same time invisible and powerful, act like currents moving "sluggishly" in line with "deeper currents in the society at large". Temporary "gusts of academic fashion" may cause ripples on the surface, but it is the underlying currents moving in "intuitive, somnambulistic" (p. 127) ways which are the most enduring. Hudson's metaphor is passive rather purposeful: far from being explorers shaping our intellectual landscape, we are helpless passengers swept along by powerful and unknowable forces.

3: Researching paradigms

> 'Methods are not simply neutral tools: they are linked with the ways in which social scientists envision the connection between different viewpoints about the nature of social reality and how these should be examined.'[16]

We've seen that explaining Fine Art at the university means looking at the assumptions behind the educational paradigm: Körner's "exhibition of implicitly accepted categorial frameworks" (Körner, 1974, p. 59). We've looked at the characteristics of paradigms. The question now is, how do we do it?

Certainly the majority of research methods are very focused on what's visible. But fortunately there are some which resist invisibility.

3.1 Soft Systems Methodology (SSM)

Soft Systems Methodology (SSM) was developed by systems theorist Peter Checkland and comes from the natural sciences, where treating living organisms as fixed subjects for empirical research clearly has its limits. For example pinning a butterfly to the wall may show us something about the butterfly at a particular moment in time, but nothing at all about its life-cycle. Similarly, investigating the molecules of an apple tells us nothing about its appleness in terms of size, shape, taste, or smell (Checkland, [1984]1998, p. 78). Natural scientists may be as interested in hard evidence as any empiricist, but they also have to take account of the hidden, invisible forces which are constantly at work shaping the natural world. Take emergence for example.

> Emergence is the reason why there are hurricanes, and ecosystems, and complex organisms like humankind, not to mention traffic congestion and rock concerts. Indeed, the term is positively awe-inspiring. As physicist Doynes Farmer observed: 'It's not magic…but it feels like magic'. (Corning, 2002, p. 2)

---

16 Bryman ([2001]2008, p. 4). Alan Bryman's *Social Research Methods* is a 748-page textbook of social science methods for university students. Given the role of textbooks in defining "the legitimate problems and methods of a …field for succeeding generations of practitioners" (Kuhn [1962]1970, p. 10), we may take Bryman's positions as authoritative insofar as they represent current assumptions about social science research methods.

SSM takes as its starting point "real-world problems in all their richness" (Checkland & Scholes, [1990]1993, p. 5) and makes use of both internal and external perspectives to investigate the complex and shifting relationships between the elements of the system the problem is part of. In this way, SSM is not so much interested in the characteristics of one particular paradigm as in how different paradigms come together in a particular system.

> What distinguishes systems is that it is a subject which can talk *about* the other subjects…it is a meta-discipline whose subject matter can be applied within virtually any other discipline. (Checkland, [1984]1998, p. 5)

Initially Checkland is keen not to be prescriptive and to call SSM an approach rather than a methodology (Checkland, [1984]1998, p. 5). However he subsequently sees value in developing a more formal version of SSM processes based on his experiences as a systems consultant (Checkland & Scholes, [1990]1993, p. 5).

The first step is to identify a "real-world situation of concern" (Checkland & Scholes, [1990]1993, p. 5) which is proving difficult to explain or manage, and to find out as much as possible about both the situation itself and its environment.

The second step consists of identifying a number of other situations, either real-world or imaginary, which are likely to be relevant. This is fundamentally subjective, a creative attempt to make the "best possible choice" (Checkland & Scholes, [1990]1993, p. 31) rather than to find the right answer. As an example, Checkland cites a case study from Oxfam, where the situation of concern is the need for Oxfam's management committee to improve its performance. Obviously-relevant systems are to do with the structure of the business: "providing relief, providing aid, running retail shops, and begging". However other less obviously relevant systems turn out to be even more useful, for example "a system to resolve disagreements on resource use…or a system to define information flows to and from the management committee" (p. 32).

For Checkland, metaphor is useful for generating examples of relevant situations, particularly where the relationship between two elements is involved: "Is the relationship between A and B like that between policeman/robber, parasite/host, husband/wife…?" (Checkland & Scholes, [1990]1993, p. 32). Naming is also important. Names should signify the core purpose of the system and take on the status of root metaphors (p. 33).

The third step in the process is to compare the real-life situation of concern with the situations which seem to have some relevance to it.

> The basic shape of the approach is to formulate some models which it is hoped will be relevant to the real-world situation, and use them by setting them against perceptions of the real world in a process of comparison. (Checkland & Scholes, [1990]1993, p. 6)

The purpose of the process of comparison is not to find precise answers. Instead, we're looking for wisdom-based knowledge which resonates with the real-world situation and lets us talk about the problem productively.[17]

The final part of the process consists of identifying ways to fix the problem situation.

A characteristic of SSM investigations is "rich picture building" (Checkland, [1984]1998, p. A16). This consists of physically sketching out the parts of the system and diagramming their relationship to each other. For Checkland these sketches work in different ways from linear language, and are better at showing complex relationships.

> The complexity of human affairs is always a complexity of multiple interacting relationships; and pictures are a better medium than linear prose for expressing relationships. Pictures can be taken in as a whole and help to encourage holistic rather than reductionist thinking… (Checkland, [1984]1998, p. A16)

Even if we find drawing awkward, Checkland encourages us to make the effort, not least because the "selection of the key features of a situation is a crucial skill in developing a picture". Using ready-made templates isn't the answer either, since using "ready-made fragments" will tend to lead to solutions based on someone else's thinking (Checkland, [1984]1998, p. A16). Rich pictures are not scientific diagrams but rather tools to promote insight and debate. As an example, Checkland describes how one particularly complex diagram showing the relationship between a health authority and its acute hospitals looked like, and became known as, "the briar patch" (p. A16). The picture became a symbol of the problem situation as well as a focus of debate, and redrawing it became a symbol of change.

---

17 Feyerabend (1975) similarly promotes the value of comparison: "A scientist…will adopt a pluralistic methodology, he will compare theories with other theories rather than with 'experience', 'data', or 'facts'… It is, therefore, important that the alternatives be set against each other" (p. 47).

3.2 Multi-dimensional grids

A related research approach which also makes use of comparison is that of multi-dimensional grids. These position paradigms in relation to each other along particular dimensions.

Our natural tendency is to think about problems in two dimensions: inside the paradigm or outside it, the same or different, right or wrong. Classicist G.E.R. Lloyd (1966) traces our preference for simple polarities back to the Greek philosophers (p. 15). Aristotle's physical theories are based on "the hot, the cold, the wet, the dry" (p. 18); his political theories centre around the polarity of democracy or oligarchy (p. 65); and Plato distinguishes between two worlds, the ideal world of forms and the human world of particulars (p. 23). Lloyd's explanation is the "fairly obvious" suggestion that "opposites provide simple and distinct reference points to which other things may be related" (p. 65).

However this instinctive tendency to think in terms of polarities has some unintended consequences. One is what Lloyd (1966) calls the promotion of "dogmatic tendencies" and the temptation to "construct simple, comprehensive doctrines on the most general, complex problems" (p. 67). Take for example the traditional distinction between qualitative and quantitative methods. While it's often useful to see them as opposites, in real life the distinction between them may be quite blurred.

Another unintended consequence is way we tend to associate positive or negative values with each pole. Although polarities are not intrinsically value-laden, Lloyd (1966) notes Aristotle's unreflective tendency to take one term or other as the obvious positive. For example heat and dryness are associated with males (as opposed to cold and wetness with females) simply because *fire* and *masculinity* have come to be regarded as the "positive or superior terms" (p. 59). Returning to the example of the quantitative and qualitative research polarity, we can see that the quantitative positions have come to be seen as superior. Feinberg (1983) observes that, in educational research generally, "the dominant tradition has attempted to understand education through methods that are employed in the natural sciences" (p. 19), while Bryman ([2001]2008, p. 625) warns students that in the paradigm wars between quantitative and qualitative methodologies the winners are likely to be quantitative, particularly when it comes to research funding. So it's not surprising that polarities have historically had their opponents: educational philosopher famously John Dewey ([1916]2007) famously argued against dualisms and all their "severe" disconnections which "violently" pull apart what should go together, for example body and mind (pp. 118-131).

As an alternative, management consultants Lowy and Hood ([2004]2010) recommend the two-dimensional matrix as a way of moving beyond simple either/or distinctions and enabling a kind of dialectical debate, where creative conflict helps to identify and to challenge assumptions as well as suggesting original approaches and solutions. The purpose of the matrix is not "to simplify the world into four finite categories" (p. iii) but to identify the most significant dimensions of the problem, its "carefully selected, primary forces" (p. 9), and create around them a "rich territory of understanding" (p. vi) which helps both to focus and contextualise thinking. In this way the matrix acts as a mapping tool which positions events in relation to each other.

For Lowy and Hood ([2004]2010), the matrix is invariably more than the sum of its dimensions. By setting up a dialectic, the matrix becomes "a dynamic structure...that brings richness, depth and a uniquely transformational power to the form" (p. 3). The inherent creative tension between the axes ensures "an open, proactive" approach which encourages complexity (p. 4), tolerates paradox and leads to more informed conclusions (p. 5). Because positions on the matrix aren't fixed, thinking about their positioning leads to new ways of looking at events and new conclusions, often characterised by their "surprising obviousness" (p. 7).

Finally, the matrix taps into the power of visualisation, "the metaphoric capacity to envision whole, complex situations and scenarios" (Lowy & Hood, [2004]2010, p. 24) rather than allowing only a single logical path as written language does. Through visualisation the matrix enables a "shift in logical levels [to] a different and higher level" (p. 25).

As an example of how the matrix works, Lowy and Hood give us the classic business owner's dilemma of investing in the business or taking the profit. Expressed as a simple choice, the decision can only be based on "fear, greed or misplaced confidence" (Lowy & Hood, [2004]2010, p. 6). Expressed as a matrix, however, two sets of choices come into play, along with a whole spectrum of options taking both possibilities into account.

3.3 Metaphor

As we saw from Checkland (Checkland & Scholes, [1990]1993), metaphor is another way of making comparisons which reveal underlying assumptions and help us towards explanation:

> Every explanation, however convincing, is merely…a comparison with something else… this is a truth about epistemology – any one thing can only be understood in terms of another. (McGilchrist, 2009, p. 117)

So any process of putting different ideas and objects together to create new insights and meanings is essentially metaphorical (McGilchrist, 2009; Lakoff & Johnson, [1980]2003; Ortony, [1979]1998). For McGilchrist, "the point of metaphor is to bring together the whole of one thing with another, so that each is looked at in a different light" (p. 117), while for Lakoff and Johnson, this "metaphoric character…is true of all abstract thought, especially science. Conceptual metaphor is what makes thought possible" (p. 123).

Ortony ([1979]1998) also highlights the association between metaphor and new thinking: "the first [theme of the book] is that something new is created when a metaphor is understood. The second is that metaphors afford different ways of viewing the world" (p. 5). So metaphor has traditionally been an important way of providing explanations for which literal terms don't already exist.

For sociologist Donald Schön, tracking the underlying or generative metaphors behind texts (Schön, [1979]1998, pp. 137-163) is one way of revealing the assumptions behind paradigms. His examples are from social policy, where identifying root metaphors can reveal unhelpful ways of thinking which can then be re-imagined by a change of metaphor. Schön takes the metaphor of the *fragmentation* of services as an example. This "most pervasive" metaphor suggests the shattering of a previous integration "like a vase that has been broken", from which the only way back is through increased coordination. But a different root metaphor might substitute *autonomy* for *fragmentation*, and lead to different solutions.

4: The Framework of Educational Assumptions

'Epistemology has been…a negative discipline, mostly devoted to saying what you shouldn't do if you want your activity to merit the title of science, and to keeping unworthy pretenders from successfully appropriating it.'[18]

The Framework of Educational Assumptions (Figure 1 below) shows what happens when the research approaches described in the previous chapter are used to uncover the educational assumptions of the university.

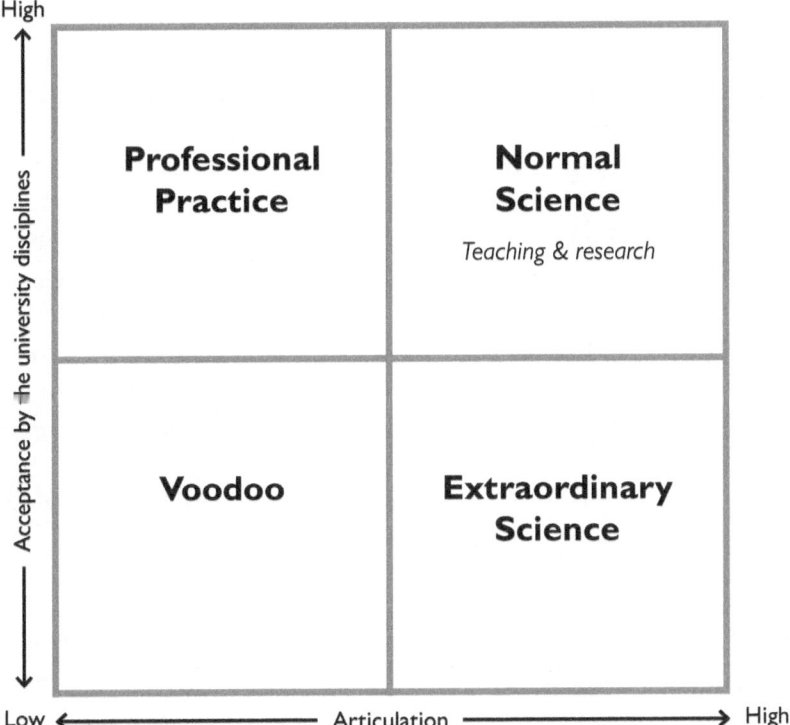

Figure 1. The Framework of Educational Assumptions.

• • • • • •
18 Bowker & Star, 2000, p. 13

Firstly, following Checkland (Checkland & Scholes, [1990]1993), we researched the literatures of art, science and education for systems which seemed relevant in some way to the field of educational assumptions. Importantly, this meant looking beyond familiar systems with an obvious relevance to the field, to consider all kinds of knowledge systems up to and including magic.

Following Lowy and Hood ([2004]2010), the two most significant dimensions to emerge from the research were then identified. The horizontal axis, *Articulation*, looks at the extent to which knowledge is articulated and in the public domain, as opposed to our private or personal thoughts or feelings. The vertical axis, *Acceptance by the university disciplines,* looks at the extent to which the knowledge is an accepted part of a university discipline.

Finally, again following Checkland & Scholes ([1990]1993) we named the quadrants to give us a root metaphor for each different part of the field.

Before we look at each quadrant in detail, let's just make some provisos about the Framework at this point. First of all, following Kuhn ([1962]1970), we take the prototype of a university discipline to be science. This may seem both unrepresentative, since university disciplines also include the arts and humanities,[19] and also imprecise, since there are differences between sciences. However there is general agreement that the science paradigm has become representative of all university teaching regardless of discipline. Art educationalist Arthur Efland asserts that "after 1957, science provided the model of curriculum reform for the whole of general education, including art education" (Efland, 1990, p. 249). So in 2013 Sir Richard Evans, Regius Professor of History at Cambridge, can begin his defence of the history curriculum by stating that "history is an academic discipline like physics or medicine" ("Michael Gove's history wars", 2013), confident in the status of physics and medicine as prototypes of the academic disciplines. So in a sense we are all teachers of science, whatever our discipline.

It's also worth noting that if Fine Art is not a science now, this was not the case historically, and the science paradigm may have an enduring relevance.

> During the Renaissance...little cleavage was felt between the sciences and the arts. Leonardo was only one of many men who passed freely back and forth between fields that only later became categorically distinct. (Kuhn, [1962]1970, p. 161)

---

19 Kuhn himself makes no claim that science is necessarily representative of all disciplines, but notes that the concept of the paradigm, and paradigm change, originates in the humanities and applies across all disciplines.

4: THE FRAMEWORK OF EDUCATIONAL ASSUMPTIONS 35

A second proviso is about the sources of evidence used to describe the paradigms in the matrix. Since paradigms are invisible and inaccessible to those who work within them, insight tends to come from outsiders.[20] Counter-intuitively, the direct evidence of practitioners within the paradigm is less reliable than the observations of those outside it.

The final proviso concerns the status of frameworks such as this. As Checkland ([1984]1998) reminds us, the question is not whether the Framework is scientifically provable, but whether it's useful.

> The...models used in SSM are devices – intellectual devices – whose role is to help structure an exploration of the problem situation being addressed. (Checkland, [1984]1998, p. A21)

With these provisos in mind, it's time to look at each quadrant in detail.

4.1 Normal Science

High articulation, High acceptance by the university disciplines

At the top right of the matrix is the core business of the university which we've named Normal Science. Kuhn ([1962]1970) uses this term to describe the routine business of the university where "the members of a scientific community see themselves and are seen by others as the men uniquely responsible for the pursuit of a set of shared goals, including the training of their successors" (p. 177). Normal Science includes both undergraduate teaching and research.

4.1.1 Normal Science teaching

Normal Science teaching at undergraduate level is about providing students with their induction into "the entire constellation of beliefs, values, techniques and so on shared by the members of a given community" (Kuhn [1962]1970, p. 175). This is to prepare them "for membership in the particular scientific community

---
20 For example Kuhn ([1962]1970) is a science historian, Schön ([1983]2007) a social scientist, Feyerabend (1975) a philosopher of science, and Brooks (2011) a science journalist.

with which he will later practice" (p. 11). Students are taught to become "inhabitants of the scientist's world, seeing what the scientist sees and responding as the scientist does" (p. 111) in a way which is both literal and metaphorical. For example, "Looking at a bubble-chamber photograph, the student sees confused and broken lines, the physicist a record of familiar subnuclear events" (p. 111).

The pedagogy of Normal Science is designed to transfer the discipline's paradigm as quickly and efficiently as possible. "Of course," Kuhn admits, this may result in a somewhat "narrow and rigid education..." ([1962]1970, p. 166), but it's also "immensely effective" (p. 164), since once students have mastered the basics of their discipline they can focus on specialisation without wasting time "constantly to re-examine its first principles" (p. 163). Teaching Normal Science involves activities such as lectures, laboratory exercises, specialized journals, and membership of societies (p. 19). For Kuhn, textbooks play a particularly important role since "more than any other single aspect of science, that pedagogic form has determined our image of the nature of science and of the role of discovery and invention in its advance" (p. 143).[21] The purpose of a textbook isn't to create an accurate historical record of the discipline, but to act as an authoritative summary of "what the scientific community thinks it knows" (p. 140).

Textbooks create a narrative of cumulative progression which show one idea leading seamlessly to another, free from the taint of "human idiosyncrasy, error and confusion" (p.138). This selective retelling gives students a sense of participating in a long-standing historical tradition and avoids the distractions which would result from including stories of "the more creative members of these various schools" (p. 10) whose ideas lie outside the main narrative. When scientific revolutions do occur, textbooks are simply revised in a way which assimilates the new ideas and makes the revolution invisible (p. 136). As a result, students rely on the authority of their teachers and textbooks rather than the original evidence itself (p. 80): "Until the very last stages in the education of a scientist, textbooks are systematically substituted for the creative scientific literature that made them possible" (p. 165).

Kuhn acknowledges that "as pedagogy this is unexceptionable" ([1962]1970, p. 140) and that its focus and efficiency has contributed to the remarkable progress associated with science (p. 152). At the same time he does worry about the dangers of such a systematic re-writing of history which fundamentally

---

21 Kuhn acknowledges that actual textbooks may be less important in non-science disciplines, but the principle of teaching consolidated knowledge as part of a seamless narrative remains the same, even if the method varies ([1962]1970, p. 165).

4: THE FRAMEWORK OF EDUCATIONAL ASSUMPTIONS

"misleads both students and laymen about the nature of the scientific enterprise" (p. 142), and in turn produces scientists who are resistant to new ideas:

> No part of the aim of Normal Science is to call forth new sorts of phenomena: indeed those that will not fit the box are often not seen at all...Normal Science does not aim at novelties of fact or theory and, when successful, finds none.
> (Kuhn [1962]1970, pp. 24, 52)

Other accounts of Normal Science note both its advantages and disadvantages in a similar way. Keen to emphasise the scientific credentials of SSM, Checkland ([1984]1998) argues eloquently for science as "probably the most powerful invention ever made in the history of mankind" (p. 24), operating as "an institutionalized set of activities which embody a particular purpose, namely the acquiring of a particular kind of knowledge" which ultimately leads to an understanding of "the laws which govern the realities of the universe, these laws being expressed mathematically if possible" (p. 50).

In contrast, science philosopher Paul Feyerabend (1975) famously denounces Normal Science as politically fraudulent, since it oversimplifies science and reduces all scientific enterprise to a uniform process governed by empiricist logic and "naïve and simple-minded rules" (p. 17). As part of this oversimplification, all wider human enterprises such as religion, metaphysics, intuitions, humour, and imagination are excluded. For Feyerabend, the tradition of Normal Science teaching may be successful, but it's also inhuman and stultifying (p. 19).

For science journalist Michael Brooks (2011), the politics of a curriculum which keeps to the rules and excludes all elements of risk or imagination is about persuading us that science is safe. As citizens of a post-nuclear society, which science has come close to blowing to pieces, we are naturally suspicious of what scientists are up to. So "all are, almost unconsciously, taught to play by a set of rules that will perpetuate the myth of the responsible, level-headed, trustworthy scientist" (p. 5). Students are forced through an exhaustive curriculum characterised by experiments which rarely work as they should. Little wonder that science is seen as a "dull, spiritless and cautious" enterprise (p. 255), and a career in science a "dull, dismal road less travelled" (p. 256). Only the most resilient and unimaginative students survive their education(p. 256), and there is a general "disengagement from science through tedium" (p. 259).

Metaphors for Normal Science teaching

Kuhn ([1962]1970) describes Normal Science without metaphor, perhaps because its characteristics are self-evident.

However educationalist Alison Cook-Sather (2003) identifies the two most pervasive and influential metaphors of education as the *production line* and the *remedial hospital* (p. 947). The production line is a persistent image in student narratives, particularly in "good" institutions.

Critics of Normal Science teaching use metaphors of taming and control. For Feyerabend (1975), scientists are "well-trained pet[s]" who conform to their masters' wishes, while science education "maims by compression, like a Chinese lady's foot" (pp. 19-25). For Brooks (2011), scientists are "wolves who have allowed themselves to be domesticated and slowly bred into yappy Chihuahuas" (p. 253).

4.1.2 Normal Science research

Kuhn's term ([1962]1970) Normal Science also includes research. He acknowledges that the layman's view is of the pioneering, ground-breaking nature of scientific research.

> Our most prevalent image of the scientist…[is of]… a man searching at random, trying experiments just to see what will happen, looking for an effect whose nature he cannot quite guess. (Kuhn, ([1962]1970, p. 87)

In the past that might well have been true. For example, Descartes was motivated by "higher-level, quasi-metaphysical commitments" to investigating the sorts of entities the universe does and does not contain, and to defining what scientific methods and solutions should look like (p. 41).

In the modern university, however, scientific research is actually very constrained. Firstly, it needs to be within the paradigm of a particular discipline. Scientific theories are usually "sufficiently open ended to leave all sorts of problems…to resolve" (Kuhn, [1962]1970, p. 10), which form the basis for further research: "…the results gained in normal research are significant because they add to the scope and precision with which the paradigm can be applied" (p. 36). Secondly, the only problems selected for research are those for which there is likely to be an answer, "esoteric" (p. 43) problems which are of significance primarily to specialists working within the discipline. This selectivity is largely responsible for the success of scientific research, since it avoids diverting time and resources into "the big questions…which…may not have any solution" (p. 37).

> To a great extent [problems with solutions] are the only problems that the community will admit as scientific or encourage its members to undertake. Other problems…are

rejected as metaphysical, as the concern of another discipline, or sometimes just too problematic to be worth the time. (Kuhn, [1962]1970, p. 37)

Finally, the success of scientific research is judged exclusively by its peers, the "professional compeers" (Kuhn, [1962]1970, p. 168) who are working within both explicit rules and a less explicit "network of commitments... conceptual, theoretical, instrumental and methodological" (p. 42). A good example is the commitment to empirical evidence , where "the dominant epistemology is of knowledge as a construction placed directly on raw sense data by the mind" (p. 96). Peer groups act as gatekeepers, allowing through only results which fit with these rules and commitments.

> The range of anticipated, and thus of assimilable, results is always small compared with the range that imagination can conceive...the project whose outcome does not fall in that narrower range is usually just a research failure, one which reflects not on nature but the scientist. (Kuhn, [1962]1970, p. 35)

As with Normal Science teaching, Kuhn can see both advantages and disadvantages in Normal Science research. In spite of, or because of, its constraints, it's very successful

> Normal Science...is a highly cumulative enterprise, eminently successful in its aim, the steady extension of the scope and precision of scientific work. (Kuhn, [1962]1970, p. 52)

Nevertheless it has its limitations, since by committing only to existing paradigms it excludes the possibility of discovering new ones.

> Perhaps the most striking feature of the normal research problems we have just encountered is how little they aim to produce major novelties, conceptual or phenomenal. (Kuhn, [1962]1970, p. 35)

In the world of research, "scientific training is not well designed to produce the man who will easily discover a fresh approach" (p. 166).

Checkland ([1984]1998) sees Normal Science research as a process of orderly enquiry into the nature of the "messy" and "mysterious" world (pp. 50-51), a process characterised by "reductionism, repeatability, and refutation". Descartes' advice "to break down problems, and to analyse piecemeal, component by component" is the watchword. The researcher's aim is to have "complete control over the investigation, so that the changes which occur are the result of his actions, rather than the result of complex interactions of which he is unaware" (p. 51). The prize is testable and objective public knowledge which is in a "different category to opinion, preference and speculation" (p. 53).

Feyerabend (1975) on the other hand is highly sceptical about the claims of scientific research to epistemological objectivity. He regards both priests and Nobel Prize winners alike as in the business of proving their theories (p. 45), and sees the emphasis on conformity as suspect, since "variety of opinion is necessary for objective knowledge" (p. 46).

Brooks (2011) is also worried by the conformity of scientific research. By insisting on playing within the rules of the game, universities have become "flooded" with "visionless scientists" producing boring research and making "mediocre, tedious advances." As an arbitrarily selected but classic example, he cites:

> ...a 2008 paper by the GEM particle physics collaboration...[which]...stretches over 20 pages, has 31 authors, and relates to the minutiae of whether a particular kind of subatomic particle called a meson forms a 'bound state' within an atomic nucleus... unfortunately, the data presented proved nothing...it is difficult to tell who would care even if further data weren't needed. (Brooks, 2011, p. 257)

Like Kuhn, Brooks (2011) sees peer review as a major form of control over the nature of scientific research. In theory, it should be an objective way of assessing the quality of submissions. In practice, since science research is highly competitive in terms of both funding and recognition, peer reviewers are unlikely to promote the interests of competitors who are a threat, either because they share their ideas or challenge them (p. 251). Researchers who are under pressure to publish are less likely to be motivated by "interesting new findings" than by "surviving the system and making sure they get enough funding to continue in their line of work" (p. 253).

Metaphors for Normal Science *research*

Kuhn's ([1962]1970) main metaphor for Normal Science research is of a puzzle where the researcher is "...a solver of puzzles, not a tester of paradigms", motivated by the challenge to their skill and ingenuity "like a chess player trying out alternate moves in the search for a solution" (p. 144). Puzzles take place in an ordered environment and can only be solved in accordance with the rules of the game, in this case "the established viewpoint" (p. 39). Importantly, they always do have a solution. Research can also be "mop up work" (p. 24), low-status tidying up after the main event of. Finally, the researcher is a map-maker, with the discipline providing "...not only ... a map but also ... some of the directions essential for map making" (p. 109). Normal Science research can discover new territory, but only within existing boundaries and using the mapmaker's instruments and methods.

Brooks (2011) cites Spanish philosopher Jose Ortega who sees the majority of scientists as "shut up in the narrow cell of their laboratory, like the bee in the cell of its hive" (p. 257). Brooks also quotes Nobel physicist Andre Geim: " 'if you follow the herd, all the grass is gone'." (p. 258).

To represent the Normal Science quadrant we've drawn images of the university's academic prizes conferred for commitment to the disciplines.

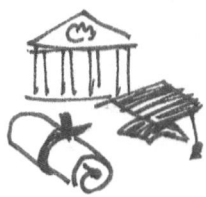

4.2 Professional Practice

Low articulation, High acceptance by the university disciplines

The top left quadrant is named Professional Practice. Here personal skills combine with theoretical knowledge from the disciplines to form the professions. For sociologist Andrew Abbott (1988), it's this linking of personal experience and competence with the academic disciplines that provides the professions with their prestige. Without it, professions will seem dubious or lightweight, and without access to new research, they risk becoming stagnant and out of date. As Schön ([1983[2007]) puts it, without a theoretical base, the work of practitioners will be no more than an avocation, based on "customary activities and modified by the trial and error of individual practice" (p. 22).

For Schön (1985) the prototypical professional curriculum consists of:

...the relevant basic science, the relevant applied science, and a 'practicum' in office, clinic, field-work or laboratory, where students are supposed to apply to everyday practice the scientific knowledge they have learned in the classroom.
(Schön, 1985, p. 5)

This is the "dominant epistemology of practice...instrumental problem solving made rigorous by the application of scientific theory and technique" (Schön, [1983]2007, p. 21).

While we can teach applied science in the same way as Normal Science, teaching competence in everyday practice is another matter, since it belongs to those "indeterminate zones of practice which do not lend themselves to the theories and techniques derived from the normative professional curriculum" (Schön, 1985, p. 5).

Schön's observational study of architectural studio teaching, *The Design Studio* (1985), focuses on the joint problems of identifying the competences practitioners need, and how to teach them. By *competences* he means the skills we use in everyday life (p. 21), tacit, implicit, spontaneous, and non-logical: the accountant reading a balance sheet or the boy throwing a ball (p. 22). For Schön, a defining characteristic of this kind of knowledge is its ability to change and adapt to events. This is knowing-in-action or experimenting on the spot, a dynamic process rather than a static acquisition of knowledge, which is subject to a continual process of adjustment or "reflection-in-action" as circumstances change (p. 28).

How then can we develop these competences in students[22]? In Schön's (1985) architectural studio, the process starts with a brief, in this case to provide a site description and the design requirements for building a school. Students are asked to develop versions of their design and record their work in sketches, working drawings, and models which are presented for critique at the end of the project to a panel of outside tutors (p. 32).

For insight into the teaching process, Schön (1985) focuses on the experience of the student Petra who is experiencing difficulties with her design. Petra shows her sketches to the tutor Quist and describes the problems she is encountering. Quist then reframes the problem in theoretical terms, while at the same time redrawing the solution. This is "the language of designing which combines drawing and speaking" (pp. 33-43). As Petra and Quist talk and draw together,

· · · · · ·
22 Schön (1985) references music conservatories, athletics training, case study teaching in management schools, apprenticeships, and the practicum of professional studies as sources of insight (p. 20). Art studios however are not included, since art is uniquely "irreducible" and "resistant to codification" (p. 11).

the design evolves iteratively through a web of moves to its final form which Petra can then take away and implement (p. 50). Schön observes how Quist is able to draw on a repertoire of similar situations he's encountered, while at the same time adapting to the new situation represented by Petra's site. This is a kind of on-the-spot experimentation "in the virtual world of the tracing paper" (p. 51). For his part, Quist sees his job as teaching his students how to "think architecturally" in a general sense. This is critical, since otherwise successful students will fail without it. Student Lauda is a case in point: intelligent and articulate, he "comes up with something that works, but architecturally it's horrible…I think he should do something else" (pp. 54-55).

For students, this kind of learning through doing is a process often fraught with "confusion and mystery" (Schön, 1985, p. 55). Much of what students think they know about design has to be unlearned to make way for new skills and perspectives, resulting in a temporary loss of competence and confidence (p. 59), but it is only by taking risks and thinking through their consequences that students will come to understand what being an architect entails. Schön sees the reflective practitioner like Quist the tutor, building a repertoire of experience and rationales to apply to new situations.

For science philosopher Michael Polanyi ([1958]1973), such personal or tacit knowledge is a necessary complement to the "impersonal, universally established, objective" (p. vii) knowledge provided by Normal Science teaching. Indeed without it, science could not exist, since "science is operated by the skills of the scientist" (p. 49) in the laboratory. However he acknowledges that such personal skills are by their nature unarticulated and notoriously difficult to define. By way of example, Polanyi reflects on what we actually know about how to ride a bicycle.

> From my interrogations of physicists, engineers and bicycle manufacturers, I have come to the conclusion that the principle by which the cyclist keeps his balance is not generally known…rules of art can be useful, but they do not determine the practice of an art; they are maxims, which can serve as a guide to an art only if they can be integrated into the practical knowledge of the art. They cannot replace this knowledge. (Polanyi, [1958]1973, p. 50)

Polanyi's appreciation of "inarticulate intelligence" ([1958]1973, p. 70) is somewhat undermined by his tendency to see its clearest manifestation in animals and children, but his recognition of the "inherently personal" character of experience, and the need to balance the tacit with the formal (p. 131) provides an influential rationale for Professional Practice.

For Feinberg (1983), the prototypical profession is medicine with its high-prestige combination of empirical science, social contribution, and personal reward, resulting in "the special status that is granted to the practising physician in all industrialised nations…college students do not generally drop out of predental programs and apply to medical school. Rather it is the other way round" (p. 175).

Metaphors for Professional Practice

Schön's ([1983]2007) recurring metaphor for Professional Practice is topographic. On the "high, hard ground" are the clearly defined problems addressed by Normal Science, while below are the swampy lowlands where problems are "messy and confusing and incapable of technical solution". The student experience is described as "swimming in unknown waters, without control, and indeed, without understanding" (p. 58).

For our rich picture of the Professional Practice quadrant we've drawn images of doctors and lawyers, the prototypical professionals.

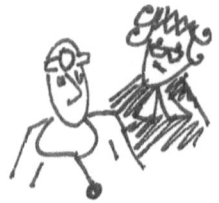

4.3 Extraordinary Science

High articulation, Low acceptance by the university disciplines

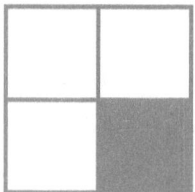

In the Extraordinary Science quadrant are the new ideas which are articulated and in the public domain but not, or not yet, accepted as part of a university discipline. The term is coined by Kuhn ([1962]1970) who argues that, while education and research are preoccupied with Normal Science, there remain real-world extraordinary problems which need Extraordinary Science to solve them (p. 34). Extraordinary scientists are not constrained by the commitments of Normal Science, but are able to see things differently. In Gestalt terms (see section 2.2) "what were ducks in the scientist's world before the revolution are rabbits afterwards" (p. 111). It's the ability to re-imagine the paradigm, to see the duck as a rabbit, that "lies at the heart of the most significant episodes of scientific development" (p. 140).

Kuhn ([1962]1970) describes how Extraordinary Science takes place against what he calls a background of anticipation, where ideas contrary to the prevailing paradigm are articulated but ignored (p. 75). So the role of Extraordinary Science may be less about new ideas and more about being able to see what is in fact already there in a process of "gradual and simultaneous emergence of both observational and conceptual recognition" (p. 62). Historical examples cited by Kuhn include identifying the nature of oxygen (p. 54), discovering X-rays (p. 57), uranium fissure (p.60), and the Leyden jar (p. 61). In all these cases, the evidence for the discoveries is available for some time in advance but remains unrecognised (p. 57).

For Kuhn, the origin of Extraordinary Science is in the "awareness of anomaly" ([1962]1970, p. 52), something which seems out of key with the prevailing paradigm. Scientists routinely resolve anomalies through the processes of Normal Science. However "anomalies that matter" are resistant to normal puzzle-solving approaches (p. 69). They may also challenge prevailing paradigms in fundamental ways, are of particular interest to society at the time, or have simply been around too long (p. 82). Extraordinary Science resolves the anomalies that matter by developing new paradigms (p. 57) through a process of trying things at random, carrying out experiments, or developing speculative theories. Even philosophical speculation, held at arm's length by Normal Science, may be involved (p. 87).

Once a new paradigm has been proposed, it has to overcome resistance to become accepted. This is typically a protracted and confrontational process for two reasons. Firstly, those committed to the original paradigm may simply be unable to see things in the new way. By way of demonstration, Kuhn ([1962]1970) cites Bruner and Postman's psychological experiment where subjects are asked to identify a series of cards which includes anomalies such as a red six of spades and a black four of hearts. In spite of the evidence of their own eyes, subjects initially identify the anomalous cards as normal. Even after coaching, some subjects:

> ...are never able to make the requisite adjustment of their categories...in science, as in the playing card experiment, novelty emerges only with difficulty, manifested by resistance, against a background provided by expectation. (Kuhn, [1962]1970, pp. 63-64)

Secondly, since the consequences of adopting the new paradigm are far-reaching, the science community must be sure the effort is worth it: "Retooling is an extravagance to be reserved for the occasion that demands it" (Kuhn, [1962]1970, p. 76). For Kuhn, this fight for acceptance is appropriate, since "no creative group recognises a category of work that is, on the one hand, a creative success, but is not, on the other, an addition to the collective achievement of the group" (p. 162).

Understanding what governs the acceptance of the new paradigm is not always straightforward however. Invariably, acceptance is about more than winning the logical argument: "probabilistic verification theories" which try to show how the new paradigm is functionally superior will probably not be enough (Kuhn, [1962]1970, p. 147). Accepting a paradigm is more a matter of belief than of logic: "persuasion, idiosyncrasies of autobiography and personality, [and] reputation" (p. 150) all have a part to play. Then there is the aesthetic quality of the new paradigm. It may simply be more attractive, neater, more suitable, or simpler than the old: "the importance of aesthetic considerations can sometimes be decisive" (pp. 155-156). Ultimately the acceptance of a new paradigm is based on faith and "future promise" (p. 158), and a gradual shift in how things are seen. When the new paradigm appears in textbooks as the latest example of progress, history is rewritten and the job of Extraordinary Science is done (p. 166).

Yet if the process of Extraordinary Science is clear from a historical perspective, Kuhn has no idea about how it happens at the level of the individual scientist:

> ... how an individual invents (or finds he has invented) a new way of giving order to data now all assembled – must here remain inscrutable and may be permanently so... (Kuhn [1962]1970) p. 90)

He can only assume that extraordinary scientists are "either very young or very new to the field whose paradigm they change" (p. 90), not yet fully constrained by Normal Science commitments. He's aware that we need to do much more to understand how people come to see things differently in the first place (p. 89), the role of intuition (p. 192), or what governs the success or failure of a new paradigm. Scientist that he is, Kuhn is hopeful of discovering an underlying rationality in the process of Extraordinary Science. For the moment, however, he has to concede that "in this area we have scarcely begun to discover the questions that need to be asked" (p. 89).

While Kuhn ([1962]1970) sees Normal and Extraordinary Science as congruent, since anomalies can only be recognised in relation to existing paradigms (p. 65), for Feyerabend (1975) they are opposed. Given the propensity of Normal Science for "epistemological prescriptions" (p. 20) in a way which is both unhistorical and repressive, progress can only come from breaking the rules, either deliberately or unwittingly (p. 23.): "even a law-and-order science will succeed only if anarchistic moves are occasionally allowed to take place" (p. 27). Feyerabend goes on to speculate about what the principles of such an anarchic science might be. For example, deduction could be replaced by counterinduction, which would deliberately introduce hypotheses at odds with well-established theories (p. 29) on the grounds that "prejudices are found by contrast, not by analysis" (p. 31). The "consistency condition" (p. 35), which requires new hypotheses to be consistent with the old, could be replaced by the principle of proliferation and variety. The resistance of science to alternatives to the status quo could be replaced by pluralism, since "there is no idea, however ancient and absurd, that is not capable of improving our knowledge" (p. 47). We could recognise that apparently factual evidence can be interpreted in different ways, and become fluent in the "observational languages" associated with different ways of seeing (p. 80). For Feyerabend, the problem is not with the rules, principles, and facts of Normal Science in themselves, but in our tendency to see them as all-sufficient and sacrosanct. We have a responsibility to "change them, create new facts and grammatical rules, and see what happens once these rules are available and have become familiar" (p. 163).[23]

Brooks (2011) contributes to our understanding of Extraordinary Science with a detailed study of paradigm-shifting scientists from Einstein to the Nobel Prize winners of the recent past. For Brooks it's self-evident that the astonishing scientific and technological breakthroughs of the twentieth and twenty-first centuries are not the result of the work of "the robot-researcher", since "you can't do good science in a straightjacket" (p. 9). Yet given what we know about Normal Science education and its focus on conformity, the questions are, firstly, how extraordinary scientists ever come to see things differently in the first place, and secondly, how they are able to persuade the scientific community to accept their version of events.

---

23 Not surprisingly, Feyerabend is believed by many to be the "worst enemy of science" (Brooks, 2011, p. 5). If by science we mean Normal Science, this is his intention.

Brooks' (2011) answer to the first question shows that the inspiration for Extraordinary Science can come from any of the zones of knowledge outside the disciplines. These include religion (p. 38), drugs, dreams, visitations, or unpredictable moments of insight (p. 39). Brooks rehearses the story of how the Renaissance scientist Girolamo Cardao is "visited by familiar spirits, angels and demons, and [takes] advice from them" (p. 29). Then there's the teenage Einstein who has a vision of running with light which inspires the theory of relativity (p. 27). Or German pharmacologist Otto Loewi whose dream of dissecting a frog's heart "brings the field of neuroscience into existence (p. 24).

The role of drugs in providing scientists with their inspiration is well-documented. According to *Nature* magazine, 20% of scientists admit to having used brain-enhancing drugs to help with their research (Brooks, 2011, p. 23). Apple founder Steve Jobs famously calls his experience with LSD "one of the three most important things I have done in my life" (p. 21), while Stewart Brand's campaign for the whole-earth photograph, "perhaps the most important endeavour that science has ever taken on" (p. 15), originates with an LSD-inspired vision. The use of drugs is interesting for the level of self-awareness it reveals in the scientists concerned. Like Hudson ([1972]1974), these people are aware of their own programming, and take deliberate steps to alter it. Interesting too is the coyness of extraordinary scientists about such experiences: "there is nothing to be gained from revealing the inspiration" (Brooks, 2011, p. 28). Even Einstein only reveals his vision at the end of his career, when it will have no effect on his credibility. In the end, inspiration is about having the confidence to believe in your own personal vision: "They just know, somehow, despite what everyone says, that they are right" (p. 259).

The second question is how extraordinary scientists persuade others to accept their ideas, given that the disciplines are constantly on their guard against accepting new ways of thinking which may prove, embarrassingly, to be wrong. A famous example is the cold fusion debacle of 1989, when two researchers rock the physics world by falsely claiming to have created energy-releasing nuclear reactions at room temperature. This is the nightmare that the science world wants to avoid at all costs (Brooks, 2011, p. 83). So it seems reasonable that new ideas should be required to prove their validity through accurate theoretical proofs, data, or experimental results that can be consistently replicated. If the evidence stacks up, so the theory goes, the idea will be accepted. If not, the ideas are wrong and will simply disappear from history (p. 74).

For Brooks, this apparently rational process works well enough for research findings within the paradigm, but "when you try to change the structure,

4: THE FRAMEWORK OF EDUCATIONAL ASSUMPTIONS

that doesn't work very well" (Brooks, 2011, p. 182). The odds are stacked against the extraordinary scientist. Reviewers of their work are committed to paradigms of their own and are highly resistant to new scientific ideas (p. 252). Ethics boards can delay or prevent work according to the political affiliations of their members (p. 104). Personal vendettas can result in "vicious personal attacks" (p. 84) and destroy careers. According to neurologist Stanley Prusiner, inventor of the prion concept behind diseases such as BSE, it seems that:

> At every crossroads on the road that leads to the future, tradition has placed against us ten thousand men to guard the past. (Brooks, 2011, p. 81).

The accepted wisdom is that this adversarial system has value, and is a significantly more powerful driver of progress than the Eastern tradition of harmony (Brooks, 2011, p. 96). Scientists themselves tend to assume that in spite of the difficulties, truth will triumph, and that, as research scientist Jenny Rohn puts it, " it is all part of the process of polishing truths out of rough ore" (p. 190).

The extraordinary scientists who win through to receive their Nobel Prizes understand the rules of the game. Since "science is a quest to convince yourself and others of something you only guess to be true" (Brooks, 2011, p. 73), it's normal to fudge the data, or at least cherry pick the most promising results (p. 51). Charisma (p. 86) and "vigorous and continuing promotion" are at least as important as the idea itself, as Prusiner acknowledges when he attributes much of his success to coining the "good name" *prion* (p. 91). Ethics committees may have to be outmanoeuvred in the name of progress (p.103), as when for example Craig Ventner uses his own DNA to kick start the gene sequencing project (p. 104). In the end, the fight is what matters: "if you want to achieve greatness in science, you need to be ready to be killed or be killed" (p. 165).

Yet for Brooks, the rules of the game can often be difficult to justify, if only because of their impact on individual scientists. Botanist and geneticist Barbara McClintock is awarded her Nobel Prize in 1983 (p. 171), but only after decades of derision during which she ceases publication and works alone for her own satisfaction. What, he wonders, goes on "inside the mind of a scientist who has climbed the biggest peak, yet has become an object of ridicule, scorn and callous snubs" (p. 178). Astronomer Chandra boycotts his own Nobel Prize party after similar treatment at the hands of Cambridge don Arthur Eddington, who, faced with Chandra's revolutionary work on black holes, "couldn't fault the mathematics, and he didn't bother to try: he simply ridiculed the basis of the idea that a star could disappear" (p. 197). As Brooks observes, "many scientific anarchists know what it is to lose everything in the pursuit of discovery" (p. 193).

Brooks also finds himself questioning the priorities of a university system which invests so heavily in resisting new ideas. The example of self-taught Stanford Ovshinsky, who changes the world and the Japanese economy with his invention of flat-screen technology, but who remains ostracized by both the Western university system and the Nobel Prize committee (Brooks, 2011, pp. 205-210), suggests that, to say the least, "we need to set up a better system" (p. 250).

In terms of teaching Extraordinary Science, it's worth mentioning the work of Edward de Bono (2009). De Bono recognises the need for business executives to be responsive to changing market conditions, and is associated with the development of lateral thinking and a series of creative thinking techniques. De Bono's tools and techniques are consistent with theories of the laterality of the brain and focus on making the shift from left-brained to right-brained thinking, but although they have accepted value for management training[24], the idea of developing logical techniques to promote non-logical thinking seems inherently conflicted. De Bono's tools and techniques have had little influence in the mainstream educational world.

Metaphors for Extraordinary Science

Kuhn ([1962]1970), Feyerabend (1975), and Brooks (2011) all use metaphors of warfare to describe Extraordinary Science.

Kuhn uses revolution as a metaphor of change ([1962]1970, p. 92), since for new ideas to survive, they have to replace those that came before (p. 98), just as "political revolutions aim to change political institutions in ways that those institutions themselves prohibit." (p. 93). This is a difficult and protracted process, where "the parties to a revolutionary conflict must finally resort to the techniques of mass persuasion, often including force" (p. 93).

Feyerabend (1975) uses the metaphor of anarchy to identify the underlying theme of his argument: "Science is an essentially anarchistic enterprise" (p. 23) which is "much closer to myth than a scientific philosophy is prepared to admit" (p. 295).

Meanwhile in Brooks (2011) metaphors of conflict abound, summarised by his conclusion that

---
24 For example de Bono's website (www.edwdebono.com) contains endorsements from Richard Branson and Nobel Prize winner Sheldon Lee Glashow.

4: THE FRAMEWORK OF EDUCATIONAL ASSUMPTIONS

> Science is a battleground. It is written in the constitution of science that the road to Stockholm will be lined with jeering colleagues. (Brooks, 2011, p. 95)

It's interesting to think about who the enemy is in these accounts. Earlier ways of thinking? Other scientists in competition or opposition? The problem for the university is that not only does it not teach Extraordinary Science, but it also seems instinctively opposed to it, in spite of its extraordinarily high value to the status of science and its inevitability. Brooks (2011) quotes Ovshinsky in this context:

> All the time they're being treated in a 'giving of information to you' kind of way, and then when they get out of school they say, 'OK, now you're on your own, think, be creative'. (Brooks, 2011, p. 257)

We've characterised Extraordinary Science by the traditional images of inspiration and genius, the light bulb and Archimedes' Eureka moment.

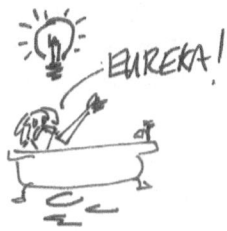

4.4 Voodoo

Low articulation, Low acceptance by the university disciplines

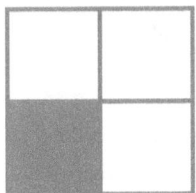

The final quadrant is Voodoo, where we find what philosopher Ken Wilbur calls the "disqualified universe" (Wilber, 1998, p. 81). Here knowledge is both unarticulated and outside the authority of the disciplines. The name comes from Feyerabend (1975) who faces criticism from a Dr. Hesse for allowing metaphysics into scientific thinking, on the grounds that we might as well "go back and exploit the objective criticism of modern science available in Aristotelianism, or indeed in Voodoo" (p. 48). This leads Feyerabend to reflect on how Voodoo has become "the paradigm of backwardness and confusion" (p. 50), representative of all that is other in relation to science and including "religion, metaphysics, intuitions, a sense of humour, imagination," and natural language (p. 19).[25] In philosophical terms, this is a world beyond the reach of logic and rational thought, which has nothing to do with the explained world. As Körner puts it:

> ... the possibility of apprehending the world without employing any categorial framework, for example through mystical experiences, will not concern us here. (Körner, 1974, p. 17)

For classical scholar E.R. Dodds (1951), this view of the irrational originates with Aristotle who's less interested in man as he is than in "the glorious picture of man as he might be, the ideal *sapiens* or sage". For Aristotle, moral perfection depends "solely on the exercise of reason". Passions are merely "errors of judgement, or morbid disturbances resulting from errors of judgement" (p. 239). If rationality is associated with perfection, irrationality is conversely associated with evil (p. 239) and "acts of cult" (p. 240): dreams, the wars of the gods, concepts of good and bad fortune and acts of public worship lose their power as the seeds of the modern freedom to choose one's own beliefs logically are sown (p. 242).

Yet as historian Charles Freeman (2003) reminds us, rationality is put on hold in the fourth and fifth centuries AD (p. xv), destroyed by the political and religious forces which made up the "highly authoritarian" government of the late Roman Empire (p. xvii). Desperate for order in a fragmenting empire, a religious orthodoxy is imposed which stifles independent reasoning, so that:

> By the fifth century not only had rational thought been suppressed, there had been a substitution for it of mystery, magic and authority, a substitution which drew heavily on the irrational elements of pagan society which had never been extinguished. (Freeman, 2003, p. xviii)

Freeman (2003, pp. 138-145) describes how early Christianity establishes its authority through the use of ritual and mystery. The scriptures are sacred and unchangeable, and only priests and scholars have the authority to interpret them. The bishops alone, as successors of the apostles, have the final say in matters of doctrine. Miracles are proof of the existence of God, and exorcisms of the

---

[25] Feyerabend (1975) goes on to argue for Voodoo as a legitimate field of scientific study (p. 50) in a way which Brooks (2011) describes as "provocative and mischievous" (p. 7).

4: THE FRAMEWORK OF EDUCATIONAL ASSUMPTIONS

existence of the devil. Faith rather than reason is the defining characteristic of the good Christian. Following Constantine, Christianity's move from being "a religion of outsiders to one of insiders" is " a transformation of incalculable importance for Western history" (p. 155) which results in "the extinction of serious mathematical and scientific thinking in Europe for a thousand years" (p. 343) until the Renaissance.

In the twentieth and twenty-first centuries, the work of anthropologists Wade Davis (1985) and Hamilton Morris (2011) in Haiti provides a fascinating and disturbing contemporary insight into the world of the irrational, and specifically into Voodoo. Morris describes how, in the 1980's, Harvard ethnobotanist Wade Davis is commissioned by the Mars space project to investigate the drugs reportedly used by Voodoo bokor to create zombies, and their potential for keeping astronauts sedated for the duration of their journey. When Davis's "swashbuckling" (Morris, 2011, p. 52) account of discovering and analysing the drug is published, however, there is "an explosion of controversy" in the scientific press and Davis is denounced as the perpetrator of a "carefully planned, premeditated case of scientific fraud" (p. 53). His story "demonstrates the strange sensitivity encountered when one provides scientific evidence for phenomena once believed to be purely supernatural" (p. 54), perhaps because to study Voodoo seriously is to acknowledge its existence in a world from which it has been disqualified.

In spite of this, Morris (2011) is keen to follow up on Davis' work by conducting his own research. His account is memorable for the way in which it conjures up the reality of an irrational world ruled by a *gros-bon-ange* life force whose ceremonies lead men to "laugh, snarl, cry, punch one another, and embrace. Children are thrown in the air…the dancing and music continue in complete darkness" (p. 56), and where a pig is slaughtered, screaming and thrashing in agony, as an act of love and tenderness, setting it on its way to the heavens as a feast for the gods (p. 57). Ultimately Morris' account, although often sympathetic, confirms our darkest fears of the unknowable worlds in the Voodoo quadrant:

> I am slowly becoming acquainted with a special kind of fear, perhaps one uniquely Haitian, that spans both physical and metaphysical realities – the fear of a world with both guns and ghosts, poisons physical and notional; fear that plagues the mind disencumbered of scientism (and accordingly allows me to truly understand the liberating power of science); the simple fear that anything is possible. (Morris, 2011, p. 58)

If Voodoo represents the fear that comes from unlimited possibilities, however, it can equally represent the excitement of the unknowable. Philosopher Nicholas Davey (2006) makes the connection between the Greek concept of *theoria* or contemplation and the way in which we experience art. Standing in front of a work of art we absorb its meaning in a state of "unreflective consciousness" which provides "an enormous vitality of potential…yet-to-be-activated meanings". As theoria anticipates the arrival of the gods in ancient Greece, so contemplation opens up a space which transcends both rational analysis and the intentions of the artist and in which an "inexhaustible" stream of ideas and emotions are provoked (p. 33). Contemplating the artwork results in "intensely personal experiences" which reveal the world to us in a new way and force us to see that "what we thought was the world was, indeed, only an aspect of it (p. 32).

Metaphors for Voodoo

Voodoo is itself a metaphor for the "occult, poetic or mythological traditions" belonging to "a superstitious, myth-laden world" against which science is the only weapon (Checkland [1984]1998, pp. 25-30).

In a curious twist, however, the metaphors of magic and religion which should belong to this quadrant have been increasingly appropriated by Normal Science. For Bowker and Star (2000), science and technology are the new magic, since "if we don't understand a given technology today it looks like magic" (p. 9). Similarly for Brooks, scientists are as magical as old-fashioned illusionists, since "when we look behind the curtain, science is astonishing" (Brooks, 2011, p. 6), and scientists are high priests, venerated "to the point of mysticism". Indeed for Stephen Hawkings, if science gets where it wants to go, it will know the mind of God (p. 10). Appropriating the metaphor of the Voodoo quadrant is a step in the right direction.

For the Voodoo quadrant we've chosen art historian Sarah Thornton's ([2008]2009) perception of how the university sees the artist, as the magical "guy who stirs the big black pot" (p. 66).

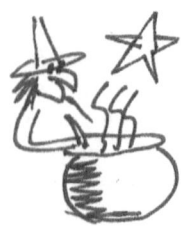

4.5 The dynamics of the Framework

Putting the rich pictures together gives us an illustrated version of the Framework of Educational Assumptions shown below. The educational paradigms of the university, Normal Science and Professional Practice, are protected by a barrier of barbed wire which is designed to keep out both Extraordinary Science and Voodoo.

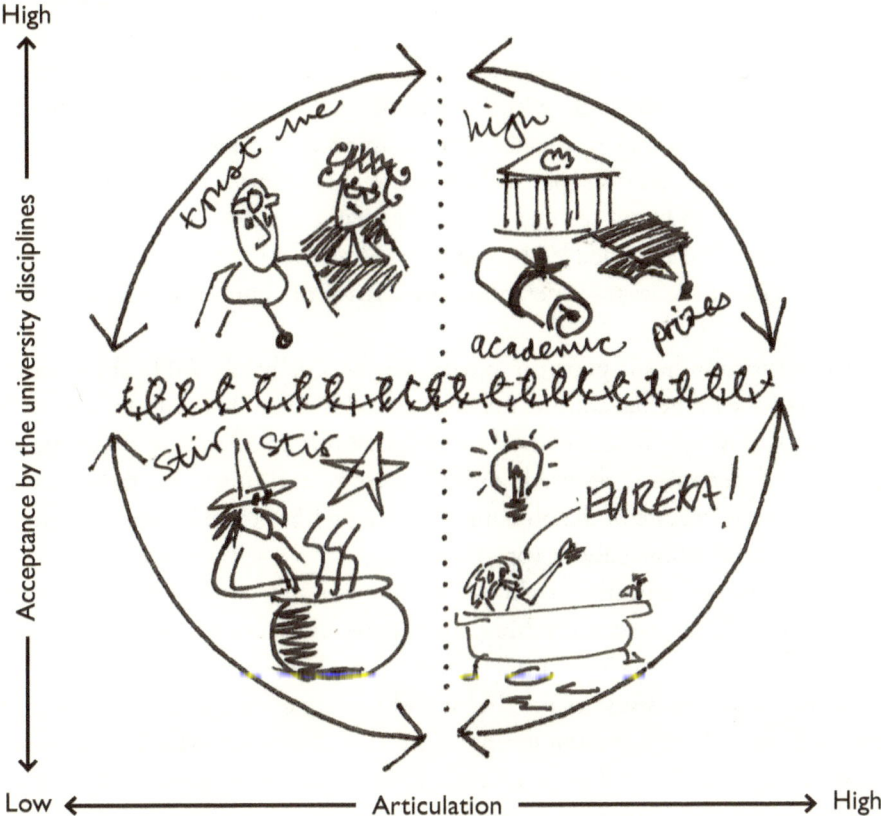

Figure 2. The rich picture version of the Framework of Educational Assumptions.

Reading the picture as a whole, we can see that the assumptions represented by each paradigm in each quadrant are different from but are also related to each other in a circular dynamic. If we move clockwise around the Framework, we can see how Normal Science is related to Extraordinary Science through a shared commitment to articulating and sharing ideas. Extraordinary Science is related to Voodoo in its openness to irrational influences, be they drugs or dreams. Voodoo is related to Professional Practice through the intangibles of tacit or unarticulated knowledge. Finally, Professional Practice is related to Normal Science through a common theoretical base. In this way we can read the Framework as a process model where the disciplines are continually refreshed by new ideas from the Voodoo and Extraordinary Science sectors, once they have been carefully evaluated in terms of their utility or validity by getting past the barbed wire fence.

If this reading is right, it also demonstrates the distortion which happens if we identify education only with the top half of the matrix and exclude the rest. This separation makes it really difficult to accommodate new ideas of any kind, and results in tensions particularly between Normal Science and Voodoo which, rather than being seen as parts of the same process, become diametrically opposed. This is evidenced by the science/religion wars in the US, and the desire, at least at the level of metaphor, for science to appropriate the quadrant altogether.

This distortion hasn't gone unnoticed. For McGilchrist (2009), it's a manifestation of the perpetual conflict between the Master and his emissary (the title of his book), where the dependent or emissary role of science to explain and illuminate experience is reversed, and a "excessive and misplaced rationalism" claims mastery, in spite of the obvious truth that without lived experience there is nothing to be rational about (pp. 1-14).

In the world of educational philosophy the relentless privileging of rational, scientific disciplines over everything else has resulted in a history of disquiet. For example Dewey ([1916]2007) argues that an educational system whose values and attitudes result in the first world war must change its "narrow and exclusive" (p. 82) aims to something more morally robust which emphasises personal responsibility[26]. Herbert Read's (1953) *Education Through Art* makes the case for art education in the early years as essential for "the reconciliation of individual uniqueness with social unity" (p. 5), instead of a system which promotes conformity at the expense of individual difference. Recently the Cambridge Report into primary education (Alexander, 2010) argues for a richer mix of educational possibilities and a more informed debate than the current naïve

---

26 For this, Dewey remains controversial: *Democracy in Education* comes in at number 5 in the top ten most harmful books of the nineteenth and twentieth century listed on the US conservative website www.humanevents.com

association of rote learning with high economic performance. However these arguments have traditionally had little traction against the status quo.

> Existing assumptions and practices are there, then, to be questioned for what they are – habits of thought and action which are so deeply ingrained that most people don't pause to think about them. Those who do question such habits are likely to be met with the blank gaze of incomprehension or with the steely dogma of 'There is no alternative'. There is an alternative of course… (Alexander, 2010, p. 17)

Philosopher Alain Badiou (2005) reflects on the ways in which distortions such as these affect perceptions of art as a discipline. There's the "judgement of ostracism" (p. 1) or the *didactic schema* (p. 2) which rejects art because it is not true in the way that science is. Then there's the "pious devotion" to art or the *romantic schema* (p. 3) which lays claim to every other kind of truth. Even the *classical schema*, which seems to reconcile the two by stating that "art is not truth, but it also does not claim to be true and is therefore innocent" is achieved at the cost of denying any kind of formal status to art, since "strictly speaking, within the classical schema, art is not a form of thought" (pp. 4-5). Badiou pleads for a new schema, a "fourth modality of the link between philosophy and art" (p. 8) which will replace the "saturated" doctrines of the past and recognise the immanence and singularity of artworks: "art is rigorously coextensive with the truths that it generates…[and]…these truths are given nowhere else than in art" (p. 9). Badiou's fourth schema is designed to reinstate the different kinds of truth which have been either diminished or rejected by formal philosophy (p. 10). Our task is now "to make them manifest (a very difficult task indeed)" (p. 15).

Part 2:
The historical perspective

5: The historical narrative

'To understand the twenty-first century, looking back at the past helps to situate our current time.'[27]

Fine Art education may be difficult to explain, but it nevertheless has a long and well documented history reflecting the socio-economic and cultural conditions of its time. If we want to understand what's happening today, we need to understand this historical narrative: what, of all the evidence, deserves our continuing attention and how it frames our current assumptions. As Pevsner (1940) observes:

> Only by throwing into relief the individual oneness of any given period or style or nation, and the logical coherence of all its utterances in the most varied fields of human activity, will the historiographer in the end be able to make his reader discover what form a certain problem must take at the present moment. (Pevsner, 1940, p. ix)

Similarly Daichendt (2010) argues for continuity between past and present, since "an awareness of the past brings to mind traditions, vocabulary, and forgotten aspects of our chosen profession as artists and teachers". For him, histories provide a rich mine of information for our "contemporary perspective[s] … to reinvestigate" (p. 3). For Elkins (2001), the obvious place to start his own investigation of Fine Art education is with its histories, since "history allows us to begin to see the kinds of choices we have made and the particular biases and possibilities of our kinds of instruction" (p. 1). Studying the past can reveal the origins of particular rituals, leaving us "free to ask whether or not other rituals might not be better" (p. 107). Elkins (2008) also sees benefits for students, since if we were to teach historical awareness as well as methods students would become more "historically reflective", able to see their education as coherent rather than "disharmonious" (p. 2).

To understand the paradigms of the past, the place to start is generally held to be Nicklaus Pevsner's *Academies of Art, Past and Present* (1940), a "work of indispensable reference" according to fellow historian Carl Goldstein (1996, p. 1). Like one of Kuhn's textbooks, this book has a particularly authoritative

---
27 Daichendt, 2010, p. 4

status as the first attempt to construct an orderly historical narrative tracing the evolution of art education in its wider social and ideological contexts. The following account is based largely on this work of Pevsner's which still remains unchallenged. Our purpose is to identify past paradigms of Fine Art education and see where they go on them on the Framework of Educational Assumptions.

5.1 The medieval workshop

The oldest paradigm is the medieval workshop, "the soil from which the greatest achievements of European art…[have]… grown" (Pevsner, 1940, p. 225).

Under the medieval system, aspiring artists are chosen at around the age of 12 to be apprentices, spending between two to six years in "low-grade labour, such as grinding pigments, preparing panels and painting in backgrounds and drapery" (Elkins, 2001, p. 7). The workshop is controlled by the master, and training consists of providing manual help with the master's jobs during the day (Pevsner, 1940, p. 38) and copying objects and artworks in the evenings (Elkins, 2001, p. 7). The workshop apprenticeship is the first stage of a lengthy induction into a guild or confraternity of craftsmen where the ultimate goal is to be designated master oneself. Belonging to the guild confers privilege, status, a sense of belonging – and even one's own exequy or funeral ode (Pevsner, 1940, pp. 34-56).

In return for status and security, artists work under considerable personal, social and economic restrictions. There's not much individual freedom: the apprenticeship tradition is one "of working under the master instead of freely studying on one's own" (Pevsner, 1940, p. 58). In fact, no one can practise as an artist at all without the permission of the guild. Pevsner gives us the example of the seventeenth century aristocrat and artist Battista Paggi, who is "persecuted…with fervent hatred" (p. 67) by the guild of painters in Genoa because he hasn't done the seven years of local apprenticeship the guild requires. Artists aren't allowed to travel (p. 82) and there are restrictions on importing works of art (p. 83) so that art patrons can protect their investment. There are academic restrictions too: artists aren't part of the universities, with the result that they're effectively "cut off from the intellectual life of their time" (Elkins, 2001, p. 8).

Although Pevsner clearly identifies the paradigm of the medieval workshop with the social and economic conditions of the time, in fact it proves remarkably enduring. In the nineteenth century, its ideals are adopted by the German Nazarene movement whose founders, Franz Pforr and Friedrich

Overbeck, argue for a return to the spirit and practices of the masters of the Middle Ages (Pevsner, 1940, p. 206). At the start of the twentieth century, William Morris's Arts and Crafts movement takes up the Nazarene case by arguing for a return to the social foundations of medieval art practice (p. 261). In his publication *Should we stop teaching art* (1911), Morris follower C. R. Ashbee (1911) claims that "the craft cannot be learned in the school, the craft can only be learned in the life of the workman in the workshop..." (p. 4), and is nostalgic for a world where art practice is socially and economically integrated as in medieval times:

> Much of the public money now spent in futile teaching might be better spent in the endowment of artistic workshops...the figures of the Royal College of Art always come back to one as a sort of refrain, 'You have taught 459 of us this thing, but only 32 of us have taken it on as a livelihood and 126 are going on teaching it.' (Ashbee, 1911, p. 26)

Even in the twenty-first century, the medieval workshop paradigm lives on in the world of commercial art production. Sarah Thornton's account of her visit to the studio of Japanese artist Murakami ([2008]2009, pp. 183-217) describes an environment where, in spite of the futuristic technology, some aspects "hark back to the painting atelier of Peter Paul Rubens" (p. 201).

Murakami's studio is a highly disciplined environment, "tidy, white walled and silent" (p. 190), dominated by the master and his temperament.

> Murakami was on his way out, having just finished his daily inspection. He looked glum...the painting assistants looked like they'd just been chastised...one of the assistants told me she had a recurring dream in which Murakami is yelling at her. 'He is always angry,' she explained with a shrug. 'The atmosphere is usually intense.' (Thornton, [2008]2009, pp. 187-188)

The process for creating commissions starts in the digital studio, where designers and animators scan Murakami's drawings and fine-tune the images until he is satisfied. The images are then sent to the painting studio where a team of assistants complete the commissions (Thornton, [2008]2009, p. 197). Thornton observes three assistants working on a triptych of circular paintings who have upset Murakami. His anger is directed at the quality of their work: black lines "not crisp enough", colours "not dense enough", and flaking platinum leaf (p. 188). Meanwhile other assistants carry out work consistent with Elkin's description of the tasks of the medieval apprentice as "low-grade drudgery" (Elkins, 2001, p. 7). These include filling in the surface of a painting with a "thin round bamboo brush", reapplying platinum particles, applying 20 layers of gesso primer to blank canvasses to make them "flat as glass", drying paint with a hair-dryer, and filling in the outlines of Murakami's trademark flower-ball pictures with the exactly the right colour and texture of paint in a way which looks to Thornton like "painting by numbers with a twist" (pp. 188-190).

A number of Murakami's assistants are artists in their own right and promoted by his company, but their work in his studio makes no use of their individual talents.

> When I asked Sati if there was any room for creativity in the work, she replied, 'None at all'...Murakami is insistent that no trace of his or any other painter's hand be seen in the work. (Thornton, [2008]2009, p. 188)

Murakami's relations with his assistants are often tense: one major work remains unfinished because "a few skilled staff walked out on Murakami at a crucial time and the project had to be put aside" (Thornton, [2008]2009, p. 189). However he believes that his hands-on style and high expectations provide his assistants with what all creative people want: the sense that they are learning (p. 197). And like the medieval workshop, Murakami's studio is ultimately a commercial enterprise. At one point Thornton notices a stack of 85 canvases leaning against the wall, on their way to becoming paintings worth $90,000 each (p. 189).

Mapping the medieval workshop

With its emphasis on craft skills and tacit knowledge, the medieval workshop belongs most obviously in the Professional Practice quadrant. The long apprenticeships, the authority of the master and the traditions of the guilds provide the rigour necessary for professional status. In this paradigm, the skill of the artist is in making and doing.

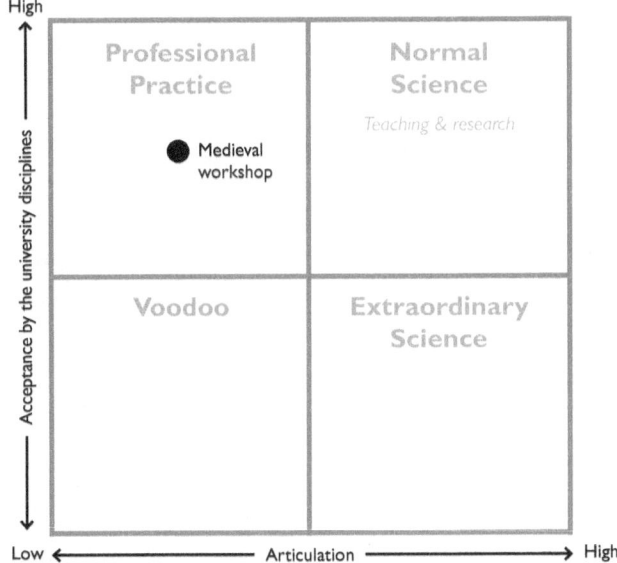

5.2 The Renaissance academy

By the fifteenth century, the medieval period is coming to an end, and the new intellectual freedoms of the Renaissance find expression in an upsurge of societies and associations where people come together to exchange ideas and pursue their interests (Pevsner, 1940, p. 8). These are the Renaissance academies.

Pevsner traces the history of the term *academy* directly from its origins in Plato's communities of philosophers to the Italian Renaissance and the "small private circles" (Pevsner, 1940, p. 3) of humanist philosophers who meet to exchange ideas and engage in speculative enquiry. As the academies proliferate, they are characterised by a surprising variety of subjects and by a distinctively informal and sociable ethos (p. 12). The earliest known association between an artist and the academies occurs in the sixteenth century with the *Academia Leonardi Vinci* (p. 25). Although the actual existence of Leonardo's academy is disputed by historians because of a lack of documentary evidence, for Pevsner this merely confirms his understanding of the Renaissance academy as "hardly more than an informal gathering of amateurs". The amateurs in the *Academia Leonardi Vinci* include "clerical and secular scholars, theologians, doctors, astrologers, [and] lawyers" as well as Leonardo himself as both artist and scientist (p. 27). In the context of the academies, art is seen as intellectual endeavour rather than craftsmanship, and painting as a form of spiritual expression rather than a manual skill (p. 33). Indeed sculpture is notoriously excluded from Leonardo's academy because "it produces sweat and physical fatigue in the workman" (p. 31). For Leonardo, artists need knowledge rather than skill.[28]

Engravings from the period provides us with more information about the Renaissance paradigm. For example an engraving of Baccio Banielli's Rome academy shows seven artists working at a long table by candlelight, with young boys learning from elderly artists, looking over their shoulders and examining statuettes of female nudes. Two youths seem to be copying the figure of a male statuette.

Although the work of copying is traditional, Bandielli's studio breaks with the medieval tradition in every other respect. The scene takes place in the evening, as evidenced by the candle, but this is not the usual kind of evening class since there is no teacher: "nothing...[is]...based on a teacher-student relationship" (Pevsner, 1940, p. 41). Instead of a master in front of his pupils, older and younger artists practise together, each studying on their own. The studio here is not so much a formal teaching environment as an informal "free gathering of men of common interests for the sake of discussions dealing with their own or other people's interests" (p. 41). "The purpose of these gatherings," concludes Pevsner "...was to enjoy in a sociable way drawing under one another's eyes and discussions on the theory and practice of art" (p. 42). In this paradigm, thinking and talking about art is as important as craftsmanship, along with what philosopher Ian McGilchrist calls respect for "personal experience, in preference to what is 'known' to be the case...for the quiddity of individual things and people" (McGilchrist, 2009, p. 328).

Just as the paradigm of the medieval workshop has survived to the present day, the paradigm of the studio as a place for students to discuss ideas as they work sociably together still has contemporary relevance.

For example a 1990 prospectus for the University of British Columbia describes a class for art students called "interactive critical analysis". The sessions are formally timetabled to take place every other week.

In all other respects, however, the sessions are informal. There is no designated teacher and attendance is not compulsory. The prospectus describes one particular session where students meet to discuss the work of one of the members of their group, which is pinned up on the wall. What follows is a

---

[28] In theory only, however. Pevsner notes that Leonardo's training of his apprentices is no different from the medieval method: "there is no proof whatsoever of any attempt of his to put into practice his ideas about the best method of instruction for painters" (Pevsner, 1940, p. 37).

discussion covering a range of themes such as the historical difference between photographs from different eras, and the way in which a historical epoch can be characterised through the poses of the people in the pictures. This discussion continues until late in the evening with only a break for coffee, and ends when the students decide. This session seems to be a direct descendant of the Renaissance academy tradition.

Mapping the Renaissance academy

Because of its interest in new knowledge across any and all fields of enquiry, the Renaissance academy seems to fit well in the Extraordinary Science quadrant.

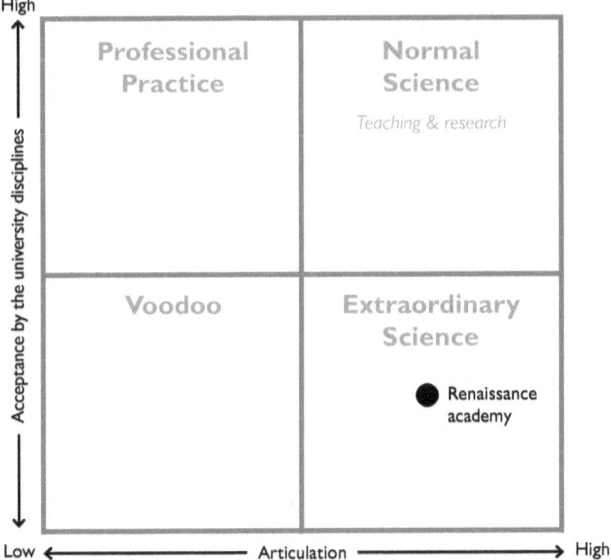

5.3 The formal classroom

The reign of the Renaissance academy paradigm is short-lived, however, and by the seventeenth and eighteenth centuries, the academies find themselves under increasing pressure to move on from their disorganised origins and adopt more formal governance structures, as the Renaissance gives way to the Enlightenment (Pevsner, 1940, p. 14).

Pevsner's history of the Florentine *Accademia degli Umidi* shows how the small art academies are affected by such pressure. The *Umidi* is founded privately in 1540 as a small and informal philological academy. It's then quickly taken over by Cosimo de' Medici, Grand Duke of Tuscany, who renames it the *Accademia Fiorentina*, revises and formalises its remit and introduces paid lecturers. In 1582, five members of the *Fiorentina*, led by the poet and dramatist Antonfrancesco Grazzini, secede because of its "solemnity and pedantry" and set up the *Accademia della Crusca* instead with no principal or fixed rules. After Grazzini's death, however, this "defence of Renaissance freedom" ends as the academy accepts the spirit of the age and reorganises (Pevsner, 1940, p. 15).

Philosopher Isaiah Berlin characterises the ethos of the Enlightenment by its acceptance of three propositions:

> That all genuine questions can be answered, that if a question cannot be answered it is not a question; that all these answers are knowable, that they can be discovered by means which can be learnt and taught to other persons; and that all the answers can be compatible with one another. (McGilchrist, 2009, p. 336)

So it's not surprising that the art schools of the Enlightenment are characterised by a series of certainties about what constitutes good art, and the intention to teach them as efficiently as possible.

Pevsner's research into this period takes him to all the major art academies of Europe including Florence, Rome, Milan, the Netherlands, Paris, Berlin, Vienna, London, and St Petersburg where he finds a "system of surprising uniformity" (Pevsner, 1940, p. 188) built on curricula that at their worst seem to him "horrifying" (p. 174). The academy has now become a classroom where attendance is compulsory (p. 61) and where students learn to draw in a series of carefully regulated stages, starting with flowers, ornaments, hands, and feet, and building up to whole figures (p. 174). Students must copy drawings before progressing to plaster casts and, finally, real life observation (p.98). Landscapes and animal subjects may be allowed as subjects, but the highest status is reserved for life drawing, with life-drawing classes monopolised by the academies in a bid for control worthy of the medieval guilds (p. 88). In addition to drawing, students are encouraged to copy "outstanding works of painting and sculpture" (p. 70) in order to develop their understanding of colour, style, and composition. These outstanding works are chosen from a "succession of masterpieces… [by]… the ancients and …modern greats" (Goldstein, 1996, p. 202) which are identified by academicians independently of the commercial art market.

The desire for rules can lead to some curious outcomes. For example, the French classical painter Nicolas Poussin issues a set of measurements for classical Greek statues so that imitations can be made with precision. And in 1708, art tutor Roger de Piles produces his "notorious" book in which "marks from

0-80 are given to all famous painters according to the value of their composition, expression, design (drawing) and colour" (Pevsner, 1940, p. 94).

Student work is assessed through annual competitions and exhibitions. Goldstein (1996) describes a typical competition conducted with "the kind of rigour associated with the nineteenth-century French academy" (p. 206). In order to enter the competition at all, students have to pass various tests in copying masterworks. Successful candidates complete a further drawing under invigilation in a two-hour period, which is then entered into the competition. Subjects are classical, for example *Alexander Cutting the Gordian Knot* (p. 206). The most successful students are awarded prizes which confer considerable prestige and are regarded as a prerequisite for a career in the academies.

Exhibitions of the students' work attract prestige for both the academies and their students. They're characterised by a certain "social glamour" (Goldstein, 1996, p. 186) and also attract the attention of the commercial art market. Sales from the exhibitions provide an important source of revenue for the academies and ensure their economic independence (p. 188).

Back in the classroom, the role of the professor is to supply drawings or casts for students to copy, set up the models, and correct the students' work. Professors rotate, for example on a monthly basis (Pevsner, 1940, p. 95), to ensure that students aren't over-influenced by any one school or personality (p. 138).

Pevsner is clearly unnerved by the classroom paradigm. The period's "unswerving...faith in clear mathematically provable rules and in arguments throughout accessible to reason " (p. 93) results in a kind of education which is "schematic and totalitarian" (p. 66) in comparison to what's gone before: "what in the Middle Ages had been the result of natural growth now became the object of conscious reasoning and methodological endeavour" (p. 138). This results in a "dictatorship of taste" (p. 103) and a cold, inhuman approach to the teaching of art.

> Rigid schemes of configuration, its distrust of the freedom of human movement, its coldness, its belief in certain teachable dogmas and certain canons discovered by a few divine artists of the past, all this goes well with absolutism and calls for an academy. (Pevsner, 1940, p. 55)

For McGilchrist (2009), the symbol of the art of the Enlightenment is the "butterfly...skewered, unmoving, a specimen in the collector's cabinet" (p. 344). In the words of artist Gottfried Schick, "the academy of art is not of live art at all, but of 'mummified' art" (Pevsner, 1940, p. 201).

If we're now "aghast" at some of the "outdated" teaching methods employed by the studios of the Enlightenment (Daichendt, 2010, p. 6), there's no doubting their continuing influence. Pevsner's own art education in Germany at the start of the twentieth century includes copying in the traditional way: "cubes and spheres in outline were still my models under an old drawing master in 1912 and 1913" (Pevsner, 1940, p. 229). Another German painter educated at around the same time describes his experiences in a similar way.

> I first learned to copy plaster ornaments in exact outline. After that I was allowed to hatch them. But this skill had first to be acquired by drawing simple cubic or semiglobular shapes…then I advanced by the death masks of Leonardo and Frederick the Great to the plaster-head of the Niobe, and via the Dying Gaul to the live model. (Pevsner, 1940, p. 230)

In the twenty-first century, drawing lessons conducted along these lines can still be found, for example as part of the evening class tradition. In one such class[29], *Drawing for beginners,* the tutor shows students how to draw eggs, flowers, hands, and the corner of the room from observation, and to copy famous masterpieces using a grid. Elkins (2001) notes that "there are still some schools that carry on these traditions…Shanghai University taught an essentially Baroque curriculum…in the United States there is the Atelier Lack…which offers a rigorous Baroque-style curriculum" (p. 199). Indeed Goldstein (1996) sounds almost nostalgic in describing an unnamed New York academy which has "a traditional syllabus organised around drawing from casts after the ancients and such moderns as Michelangelo, and drawing from live models" (p. 298) and is reputedly the envy of many art departments.

In all such classes, the spirit of the Enlightenment lives on.

Mapping the classroom paradigm
The paradigm of the classroom fits neatly into the Normal Science quadrant, with its emphasis on formal teaching, conformity, and glittering prizes.

---

29 A class I attended.

5: THE HISTORICAL NARRATIVE 71

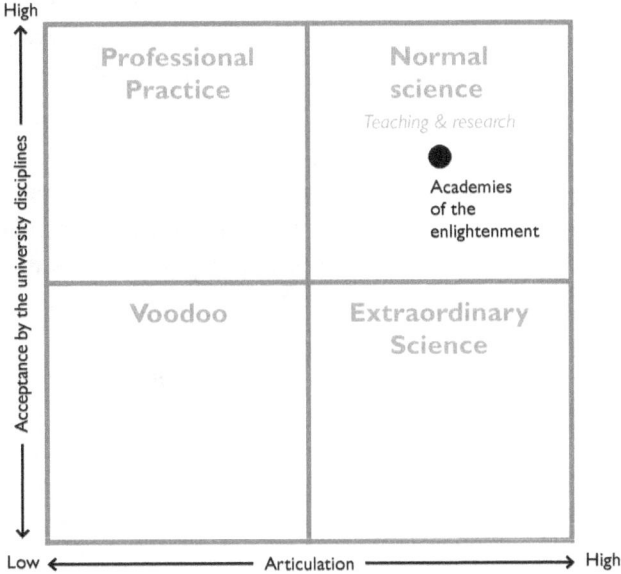

5.4 The masterclass

By the nineteenth century, a reaction to the Enlightenment's "more damagingly simplistic notions" (McGilchrist, 2009, p. 352) has set in, and the Romantic movement attempts to restore vitality to the deadened world of reason (p. 355).

In the art academies, the teaching of "mere deftness…[or]…manual skill" (Pevsner, 1940, p. 147) is now rejected in favour of real-life experience and inspiration. The idea of the artist as genius emerges strongly to the extent that for Pevsner "genius is the magic word of the young generation" (p. 190).

This new emphasis raises the rather difficult question of how to teach genius. The answer for the art schools of this period is to bring genius into the academy by replacing career academicians with famous artists, "great masters" who can lay claim to "real genius" (Pevsner, 1940, p. 209). Formal drawing lessons are replaced by "Meisterklassen… the most important innovation in the history of art academies during the nineteenth century" (p. 213).

In the masterclass paradigm, students work intensively with the master both to understand what it is to be a genius and to develop their own potential. The relationship with the master is at the heart of the paradigm. The master is a pastoral figure who will cultivate "friendly and intimate" (Pevsner, 1940, p. 205) relationships with his students and provide "fatherly care" rather than "academic routine" (p. 210). Students learn through workshops or life-drawing classes with the master, often late into the evening, and by studying nature rather than existing models (p. 212). As students begin to develop their own styles they can set up studios alongside the master, forming a community of practice.

The idea of students learning from a master artist isn't new and is indeed part of the medieval paradigm, but its incarnation as the masterclass extends and generalises the relationship. The individual genius of any particular master is now part of a wider system of many masters from whom students can choose to learn in the way that fosters their own talent best.

As with previous paradigms, elements of the masterclass have continued into the twentieth and twenty-first centuries.

In the twentieth century, artist and teacher Thomas Rehberger (ElDahab, 2006) experiences the masterclass system as a student at the Staedelschule in Frankfurt am Mein. Here students can choose their own master. Initially Rehberger choses Thomas Bayrle because "at the time I thought he was the most interesting" (p. 3). Bayrle is an enigmatic figure who is "precise and vague at the same time – he could be very hard to understand", but who Rehberger personally finds inspiring: "…it was extremely constructive" (p. 4). Bayrle then leaves for a year and Rehberger joins guest professor Martin Kippenberger's class. Kippenberger is a different kind of master, intense and demanding: his class is "very much like a sect" (p. 4), and there is pressure to think in a certain way: "…he wouldn't allow you to think about things in a way that was different to his own" (p. 5). Kippenberger has no sense of boundaries in relation to his students, engaging freely with their personal lives: "he would tell you something like 'you should leave your girlfriend because you're an artist and you shouldn't have one', or something really related to your personal life" (p. 5). Equally Kippenberger shares his own social circle of artists and friends with the students. He'll "drag" the students to a gallery opening or a museum and end the evening talking over dinner with both the students and his friends. When Kippenberger's contract with the Staedelschule comes to an end, he continues to meet up with his students just the same, since "…it was never just teaching. It was not about the institution" (p. 5).

On reflection, Rehberger feels ambiguous about the relationship. Kippenberger "was the father, and you don't question the father" (ElDahab, 2006, p. 6), but his paternalism wasn't always easy to handle.

It was definitely a great time, but it had this other side to it, a difficult side…he used us, and we wanted to be used because we thought we could get something out of it. (ElDahab, 2006, p. 5)

Rehberger is now a teacher himself at the Staedelschule. He is protective about his students "because this is a school and it's a protective place" (ElDahab, 2006, p. 1), and his relationship with them seems personal: "I have always begun with the individual student" (p. 2). However he recognises that his teaching isn't always easy for students to understand, and has its own dark side: "I destroy a lot of things…you have to be really hard to them too, but this is also about how seriously you take them". Ultimately his job is to produce good artists who will "do what they think is really important and not what they have been educated to think is important", which means that he can justify whatever methods he thinks will be most effective (p. 1).

Mapping the masterclass

The masterclass has a definite flavour of Voodoo with its emphasis on genius, intuition and originality. If Voodoo has a dark side, so too does the paradigm of the masterclass where nothing is off limits in the search for personal integrity.

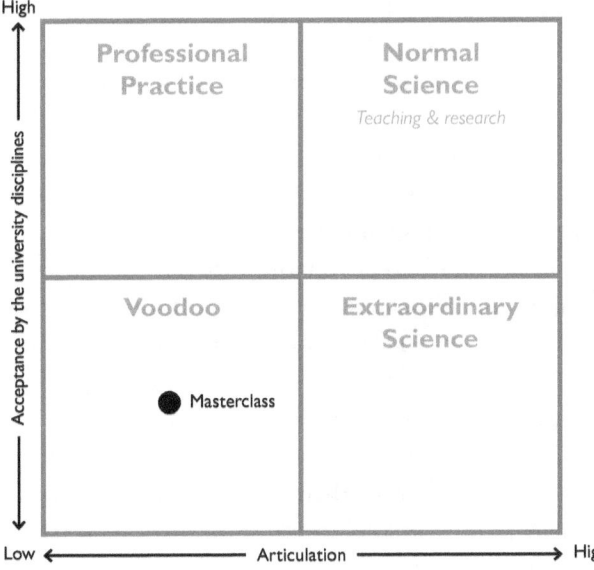

5.5 The modernist studio

The final paradigm in Pevsner's narrative is the modernist studio developed by the Bauhaus.

The history of the Bauhaus is well-known and well-documented. Established in Germany in 1919 by Walter Gropius, its initial remit is to revive the ideals of the medieval workshop. Gropius' 1923 pamphlet *Idee und Aufbau des Staatl. Bauhauses* emphasises the importance of practice over theory and calls for close links between the artist and "the realities of matter, technique, economy" (Pevsner, 1940, p. 277). Students in the workshops are supervised by one or more masters as they progress through a series of graded certificates at increasing levels of technical difficulty and specialisation. In this way the Bauhaus curriculum brings together academic teaching and studio practice in a fusion of old and new which seems to Pevsner nothing less than "a work of creative genius" (p. 279).

For art theoretician Thierry de Duve (1994), what's different about the modernist paradigm is its rejection of the idea of artistic talent as "a gift of nature" (p. 23) in favour of the concept of a universal creativity with which everyone is endowed and which can be taught as a kind of visual literacy. Gestalt theory and the psychology of perception provide a scientific basis for this approach, in that they establish that "the ability to perceive is, by nature, already cultural". Perception is a "basic reading skill" and imagination "a basic writing skill of sorts". As evidence, we can see how children have an unspoiled endowment of creativity which is largely lost by cultivated adults. So in the Bauhaus studios, students are taught the "visual alphabet and syntax" of materials, which enables them to "read their medium, obeying its immanent syntax" and produce new kinds of artworks which reflect their feelings and emotions (p. 25).

Yet it has to be said that accounts of artist Johannes Itten's teaching have more than a little of the flavour of the masterclass about them. Itten is described as taking on the role of "high priest…demonic…[and] impossible to ignore". For his followers, he exudes "a special radiance…one was inclined to approach him only in whispers; our reverence was overwhelming" (Hochman, 1997, p. 115). However Itten's intention isn't to impart his particular genius but, on the contrary, to put his students in touch with their own, through unlearning "virtually everything [they] had learned before" from traditional art teaching and regaining a sense of "childlike innocence". Itten's classes could last up to eight hours and represented "an intense and gruelling experience" (p. 116), as remembered by artist Paul Klee.

Then he talked a bit about wind, let a few students stand up and describe their impression of wind and storm. After that, he gives the task: the presentation of a storm. [After ten minutes] time [he] checks their results, holding forth in criticism. After this critique they work on them further. One page after the other is ripped up and falls to earth. Some work with such great force that they use several pages of paper at once. After they have all become somewhat tired, he has the beginners take this assignment home with them for further work.
(Hochman, 1997, p.117)

Klee's account is a good illustration of both what de Duve calls the modernists' "inward" preoccupation with "the honesty with which the artist yields to…the medium" and the role of psychology as the "foundational discourse for a new artistic humanism" (de Duve, 1994, p. 24).

Although as we shall see in the next chapter the Bauhaus fails as an institution, its paradigm of the modernist studio, "more or less amended, more or less debased" continues to be hugely influential, "still underlying, often subliminally, almost unconsciously, most art curriculums" (de Duve, 1994, p. 26).

This influence is evident in the one-year art foundation course introduced in the 1960's following the Coldstream reforms of art education, which is based on the Bauhaus preparatory class taught by Itten, itself "extraordinarily influential in modern art instruction" (Elkins, 2001, p. 32). Learning a "canon of techniques" in this way may not be very interesting in itself, but it provides students with a kind of grammar which is a prerequisite for what follows (p. 57).

Following the foundation course, the three-year degree programme is designed to help the student "to discover himself, by discussion, by encouragement, and technical know-how…to educate himself" (Kestelman, 1973, p. 46). The emphasis is on natural development, with "the artist free to explore or liberate a world of intense inner life…powerful inner confusions…producing tension" (p. 49). Such exploration goes hand in hand with the development of competence in the manipulation of visual symbols, since "the artist works in a world of visual symbols or suggestions, in terms of colour, shape, light, rhythm – the whole range of visual language" (p. 50). An important part of promoting the students' internal world is by removing conventional ideas which get in the way: Kestelman quotes the painter DuBuffet who suggests that tutors "should empty heads of all the rubbish which clutters them up. We should methodically develop, by suitable exercises, the refreshing faculty of *Oblivion*" (p. 52).

In the modernist studio, students work on their own projects which are from time to time presented to tutors and other students for critique as part of an iterative process of development. A final assessment takes place when the students' artworks are formally presented to the examiners. For Elkins, the resemblance of this process to the preoccupations of the Bauhaus is striking, suggesting that "we have moved only baby steps from the Bauhaus" (Elkins, 2001, p. 39).

Yet ultimately for de Duve, the paradigm of the modernist studio has had its day, based as it is on a philosophy which is "a biased one and a dated one" (de Duve, 1994, p. 26). Whatever its historical role in introducing modernism to the curriculum, by the late twentieth century it has become "obsolete" and "in open crisis" (p. 27), raising the question of what comes next. This is not a question de Duve feels qualified to answer, or at least not positively: art historian Lisa Tickner notes that "this is where de Duve leaves us, with no solutions and in some despair" (Tickner, 2008, p. 92).

Mapping the modernist studio

The modernist studio is the most difficult to fit in any one section of the Framework. At the Bauhaus, the early focus on craft skills and hand work puts it in the Professional Practice quadrant; teaching by master artists such as Itten is reminiscent of the masterclass and the Voodoo quadrant; the wide-ranging curriculum which crosses the disciplines fits with Extraordinary Science; while the interest in theories of symbols or colour fits with the kinds of taxonomies typical of Normal Science. For this reason we've put the modernist studio right in the middle of the Framework where it can relate to all four quadrants.

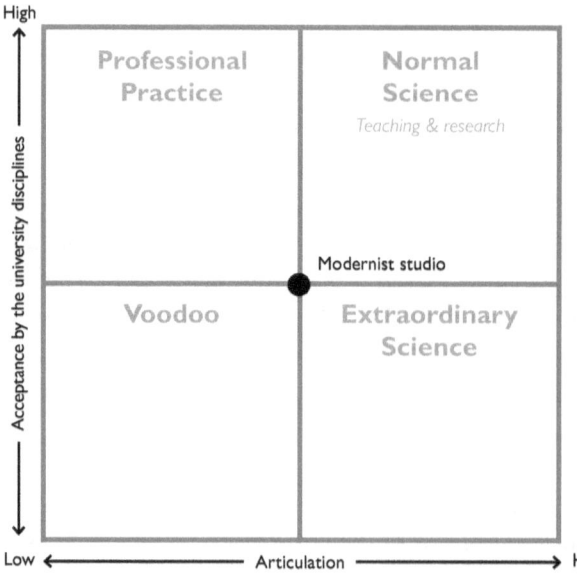

6: Interpreting the historical narrative

'Of course, one question comes up again and again: Can you claim you are anti-institutional, and yet work for one of the pillars of the system? A little hypocritical perhaps?'[30]

6.1 Traditional interpretations

Narratives of the kind constructed by Pevsner adopt what Wilber (1998) describes as the "modern … idea of history as evolution". According to this view, society is "in the process of growing toward [its] highest potential". This is the rationalist interpretation which sees history as a movement over time from the darkness of ignorance to the light of knowledge and the *summum bonum* representing the fulfilment of our human potential (p. 103).

According to this perspective, primitive medieval workshops give way to the superior paradigm of the Renaissance academy and so on, until the most highly evolved paradigm is reached sometime in the future. This is certainly Daichendt's (2010) perspective when he refers dismissively to the "dinosaur" École des Beaux-Arts as an "outdated model" for "the highly conceptual and enlightened society that today's artists must navigate" (p. 6), confident that "…the arts have the ability to shift and adjust to change, a great strength that ensures art… education will always be a service to society" (p. 21).

There is something of this confidence in Pevsner's account, most obviously in the story of how artists and their institutions develop from their humble beginnings in the medieval guilds to the Royal Colleges in the 18th and 19th centuries and the well-established art schools of the twentieth century.

6.2 Problems with traditional interpretations

Yet impressive as Pevsner's narrative is in its scope and coherence, we have to acknowledge that it raises as many questions as it answers.

------

30 ElDahab, 2006a, p. 3

Take the direction of the narrative for example. We've seen that the direction of the narrative seems evolutionary, moving from darkness to light. At the same time, however, there are also indications of the opposite view. This is what Wilber (1998) describes as the premodern idea of *deus abscondus* or the devolving world, according to which "each era becomes darker" (p. 103). From this perspective, the past is a golden age which moves further away over time, and which constantly has to be recovered.

Pevsner (1940) is often nostalgic for the paradigms of the past, or aspects of them, such as the social usefulness of the guilds or the excitement of the Renaissance academies. But paradoxically he has little time for the era which is, in evolutionary terms, the most successful. Colbert's *Académie Royal de Peinture et de Sculpture* in the seventeenth century which is tied "firmly to the court and the central government" (Pevsner, 1940, p. 109) represents a high point in the history of influence and prosperity of the academies. This success however comes at the cost of a kind of regulation which he sees as regressive: "Colbert's plan had not been looseness but tightness, not tolerance but dictatorship. This is what made his academy" (p. 108). Here art education seems to simultaneously evolve and devolve, suggesting a complex and contradictory relationship with the ideology of progression.

For Goldstein (1996), the problem with Pevsner's (1940) account is its failure to tackle some of the most difficult and enduring questions about art education. While Goldstein accepts *Academies of Art* as an "extraordinary achievement" of scholarship which defines the field (p. 1), he cannot help noticing its failure to deal with what he calls the "problematics" (p. 5) of Fine Art teaching, and in particular with "the single question that has haunted the history of teaching art from the Renaissance to the twentieth century ...precisely what should be taught and whether the essence of art can be taught, or can art be taught?" (pp. 4-5). Adopting a linear, evolutionary approach results in only a partial narrative which fails to accommodate "the complex, often apparently paradoxical nature of reality, an acceptance of the *coniunctio oppositorum*" (McGilchrist, 2009, p. 293).

6.3 The paradoxes of Fine Art education

Before we look in more detail at the paradoxes that (to use Goldstein's word) haunt the narrative of Fine Art education, it's useful to think about the nature of paradoxes and how they arise.

6: INTERPRETING THE HISTORICAL NARRATIVE

If we take the definition of paradox as propositions which are make sense in themselves but which contradict each other, we can see that they shouldn't exist in a purely rational world where everything is properly ordered, all knowledge is classified according to the laws of non-contradiction and no contradictions are possible (McGilchrist, 2009, p. 223). For this reason the fact that paradox and ambiguity do exist is a recurring source of "intellectual disquiet" (p. 137) in the Western philosophical tradition, since they suggest flaws in our ordering of the universe, "sign[s] of error" (p. 200) which are, additionally, difficult to articulate and explain.

But such an orderly world without contradictions can only exist in artificially restricted environments such as science laboratories. In the real world, we constantly make use of different paradigms based on different underlying logics which, as we have seen, are incommensurable and result in paradox whenever they encounter each other. So paradox is not only "logically valid" (Körner, 1970, p. 10), but also a natural part of our experience. As McGilchrist (2009) observes, "the real world isn't the way it is *because logic says so*…in the lived world…opposites are not 'in opposition' " (p. 140).

So in any real-life endeavour such as education we can expect that a certain amount of paradox will be inevitable. In Fine Art education, the proliferation of paradoxes gives the impression of big ideas jostling together and goes some way to explaining the high-energy rhetoric associated with it, for example when Elkins (2001) declares that "teaching in an art department or art school is the most interesting activity that I know" (p. 190), or when the Raqs Media Collective (2009) describes the work of the artist in navigating knowledge as a journey across troubled seas:

> If the work is a boat, the artist-interlocutor is a sailor…the artist takes responsibility for the safety and integrity of the work during this voyage, making sure that it lands on some more or less secure promontory of meaning before embarking on other journeys. (Raqs Media Collective, 2009, p. 80)

So what are the paradoxes of Fine Art education?

6.3.1 The pedagogical paradox

As we've seen, the idea of whether art can be taught is, according to Goldstein (1996), the central paradox of art education: although art is taught it may not be possible to teach it, in any century or by any method. Even the Bauhaus believed that "art cannot be taught" (p. 293), and with the publication of Elkins'

Why art cannot be taught in 2001, both the phrase and the concept have become common currency.

The logical response to this paradox might be to stop teaching art at all, and art tutors have been known to advise their more talented students to bypass art school since it's unlikely to improve their artistic chances. Goldstein (1996) recalls his tutor Ad Reinhardt's advice: "…when I was in his painting class in the late 1950's he would advise students who showed real talent for painting to leave school, rent a space among artists – and paint" (p. 293). Or as De Kooning famously advises his students at Black Mountain College: "I told them if they wanted to be artists, they should quit school and come to New York and get a studio and start painting" (Katz, 2003, p. 82).

6.3.2 The performance paradox

The performance paradox reflects the fact that the most successful art students don't necessarily become the most successful artists. As evidence of this, Goldstein (1996) looks at the progress of prizewinners from the eighteenth century *Academia di San Luca*. For the contest of 1702, the subject is a painting of the *Massacre of the Innocents*, for which one first prize and four second prizes are awarded. However although the names of the students who win these prizes are known, as artists they "are all difficult to trace", since "they had neither the superior talent nor, one imagines, the ambition that were the prerequisites of success in the art world of the eighteenth century" (Goldstein, 1996, p. 208). The same can be said of all prize-winners at the academies from the seventeenth to the nineteenth centuries, who, in spite of their status as stars of the academies' exhibitions, are now virtually unknown as artists. Nicholas Poussin (1594-1665) is the exception that proves the rule, the only academy prizewinner with paintings in the National Gallery.

Of course, it could be argued that the failure of the academies' prizewinners as artists represents the failure of a particular kind of teaching, and that it's the flawed paradigm of the classroom, the paradigm that Pevsner finds so uncongenial (Pevsner, 1940, p. 174) that results in such mediocre artists.

For Elkins (2001), however, the problem lies not so much with a particular style of teaching as the innate conservatism of students and teachers in educational settings. In the real world, work which is "unusual, adventurous, strong, [and] challenging" is valued, but "what is done in art classes is necessarily, unavoidably more complacent, retiring and even timid than the 'monuments' of culture and the 'masterpieces' of art history survey texts" (p. 68). Inevitably most student work will be "average and uninventive" (p. 68), "normal and low-energy" (p. 69).

The performance paradox also seems to apply to academic achievement. Following the introduction of academic entry requirements for the Diploma in Art and Design (DipAD) in 1965, a report from 1972 shows a negative correlation between success in traditional examinations and in the DipAD: "those who had failed their DipAD had the highest average in O level results, and those who obtained a third in their DipAD had achieved the highest A level results when at school" (Woodham & Lyon, 2009, Chapter 6, paragraph 11).

As Thornton reflects:

> A good artist and a good student are by no means the same thing. Art students have a reputation for acting out. Recruited for their rebelliousness, for their portfolios that are off the wall, they can be tricky for the institution to handle. (Thornton, [2008]2009, p. 65)

6.3.3 The relationship paradox

Related to the performance paradox is the relationship paradox whereby artists both embrace and reject their art schools with equal passion.

Historically there's a long tradition of artists at war with their institutions. Pevsner (1940) uncovers a whole history of documented dissent, starting in the eighteenth century with German artist Asmus Jacob Carstens. Carstens' letters constitute "the first comprehensive criticism put forward by the artist against the academic system" (p. 195). Pevsner can only conclude that, talented although he is, Carstens is too resentful of the "academic and official attitude" of the academics (p. 195) to succeed within the system. In the nineteenth century, highlights of dissent include:

- Artist Benjamin Haydon's attack on his alma mater the Royal Academy which he accuses of "meanness, fraud, and all kinds of knavery" (p. 235) and of not doing enough to "foster the grand style" (p. 236)
- Artist and poet Edward Lear's declaration that "I wish the whole thing were abolished, for as it is now it is disgraceful" (p. 237)
- Artist and critic Roger Fry's reference to the studios at the École des Beaux Arts in Paris as "the most admirably equipped…laboratories for inoculation against art" (p. 238)
- Artist James Whistler's witticism, "whom the Gods wish to make ridiculous, they make Academicians" (p. 239)

- Gasquet on Cezanne: 'He detested public art schools all through his life' (p. 239).

In the twentieth century, industrial designer Misha Black carries on the tradition when he reflects that:

> Most of us who went to art schools in the 1930's despised them as making no contribution to our development, and we attended only for the friendship of a few dedicated tutors and for the working space they provided. (Black, 1973, p. 30)

For Pevsner this tradition simply reflects the general inability of artists to behave themselves, and his sympathies are clearly with the academies as they struggle to manage such difficult, ungrateful personalities. For example he describes Carstens' letters as "self-possessed and hastily written", in contrast to the "restrained yet sincerely indignant " replies of administrator Heinitz (Pevsner, 1940, p. 196). In fact he dismisses as "a strange whim of history" the important insight that "denunciations" occur in relation to every paradigm.

> It seems a strange whim of history that all those denunciations – trade, not art; compulsion, not freedom; routine, not genius – which the first academicians and their forerunners had poured out over the guilds were now heaped upon the academies. (Pevsner, 1940, p. 204)

Yet even as they reject them, artists depend on their institutions for recognition and employment. Even the rebellious Carstens expects to be employed by the academies, to Pevsner's surprise (Pevsner, 1940, p. 197). As we saw in C.R. Ashbee's (1911), account of students at the Royal College of Art, (1911), 126 of the RCA's cohort of 459 students (27%) plan to become art teachers. In the same way, at the Frankfurt Staedschule, Rehberger's tutor Kippenberger:

> …was always – almost paradoxically – raving about the school. He was always saying what a stupid thing it is to have an art school, but then when we would go to New York with him he would be super proud, almost childishly proud, to present his students, and he is the professor. It was kind of a paradox. (ElDabab, 2006, p. 5)

Artist Robert Rauschenberg's experiences of Josef Albers at the Bauhaus encapsulate the paradox at a very personal level.

> Albers was a beautiful teacher and an impossible person… He wasn't easy to talk to, and I found his criticism so devastating that I never asked for it. Years later, though, I'm still learning what he taught me. (Goldstein, 1996, p. 283)

6.3.4 The institutional paradox

Another paradox which emerges from the narrative concerns the inverse relationship between the stability and formality of the art school as an institution and its success in producing successful artists. Traditionally the purpose of institutions is to promote the activities they wish to affirm. Sociologist Max Weber makes the association between bureaucratisation, categorisation, and power (McGilchrist, 2009, p.320), from which it seems reasonable to expect that the more focussed and powerful the institution, the more successful it will be in promoting the activities it supports. Yet as we've already seen in *The performance paradox* above, this doesn't seem to be the case with art schools.

In fact historically, the institutions of art are hard to categorise at all, as evidenced by the very diversity of terms used to describe them: "workshop, club, school, and academy" (Goldstein, 1996, p. 10). Pevsner (1940) focuses on the academies as the most knowable of the institutions, but even here is met with uncertainty at every turn. His starting point, after all, is the *Academia Leonardi Vinci*, which, as we have seen, may or may not have existed. As Goldstein admits, "despite all this attention, the academy as a teaching institution has remained highly elusive" (Goldstein, 1996, p. 3).

When during the eighteenth and nineteenth centuries the major European art academies do start to emerge more clearly and to acquire unprecedented power and authority (Pevsner, 1940, p. 108), it's precisely these institutions that are responsible for what is now generally regarded as "the failure of academic teaching" (Goldstein, 1996, p. 3).

To understand more about this paradox, we can look at two of the twentieth century's most influential and documented art institutions, the Bauhaus and Black Mountain College.

The Bauhaus

Throughout her account of the Bauhaus, historian Elaine Hochman (1997) struggles with the paradox of an institution which is at once brilliant and fatally flawed in a way which reflects the personality of its founder, Walter Gropius. On the one hand, Gropius shows extraordinary will and drive in establishing and directing the Bauhaus (p. 161). The school has an unprecedented community spirit and Gropius himself inspires personal loyalty through his "idealism, enthusiasm, and tenacity…[and]…his warm, magnetic personality" (p. 186). His vision of "an artistic style … defined by rationalistic traits" (p. 249) is taken up by "messianic" American followers for whom the Bauhaus is "the most influential experiment in artistic education" (Bergdoll & Dickerman, 2009). This in addition to its extraordinary architectural legacy (Hochman, 1997, p. 160). It's fair to say that in the literature of the Bauhaus its legacy is generally described in exemplary terms, a radical experiment gone right.

And yet in reality the Bauhaus is characterised by a series of contradictions. It's an art school established by an architect, whose "real heart" lies in architecture but whose institution does not teach it (Hochman, 1997, p. 161). It believes that art can't be taught but employs internationally recognised artists, for example Itten, Moholy-Nagy, Kandinsky, and Klee (p. 161). Although it's committed to the philosophy of industrial design, its 1923 exhibition shows mainly "terra-cotta pots…whose tormented forms made them unsuited for mechanical reproduction" (p. 160). Gropius' leadership is enigmatic to say the least, since "what Gropius wanted no one knew" (p. 185). His inability to attend to the detail of running the school periodically threatens its survival and contributes to a general air of crisis and instability.

Gropius lasts nine years at the Bauhaus, which itself survives for only 14, closing in 1933 as the Nazis come to power. Yet in assessing the legacy of the Bauhaus, Hochman comes to the realisation that the contradictions are important, and that the very qualities that precipitate its downfall are essential to its success. Ideologically, Gropius' tolerance of uncertainty, his ability "to leave everything in suspension, in flux" (Hochman, 1997, p. 219) results in a serenity at the centre of the Bauhaus which allows diverse views to co-exist. Indeed Anni Albers sees Gropius' main contribution as the maintenance of a "creative vacuum" (p. 219) for others to fill. Institutionally, the vacuum leads the Bauhaus to appear conflicted, chaotic, and difficult to categorise: "the question [is]… whether the Bauhaus was a workshop, school or academy" (Goldstein, 1996, p. 201). All that can hold such diversity together is the energy of Gropius, the "truly driven man" (p. 219). If the narrative of institutions is that the organisation is greater than the individual, the reality of the Bauhaus is that the individual *is* the organisation. Gropius' successors have to begin again with their own vision involving, in the case of Mies van der Rohe, expelling the students (p. 246). In the event, Pevsner's insight seems right, that "a school such as the Bauhaus…can – of course – only be successfully run by one strong personality" (Pevsner, 1940, p. 295).

The troubles at the Bauhaus are amplified by its historical context and the political instability of the inter-war period, yet for de Duve "the Bauhaus…died under the pressure of its own contradictions as much as it did under the hand of the Nazis" (1994, p. 26). The subsequent history of Black Mountain College in the US seems to support this view.

6: INTERPRETING THE HISTORICAL NARRATIVE

Black Mountain College (BMC)

In 1933, former Bauhaus teacher Josef Albers is recruited to lead Black Mountain College (BMC), an experimental institution for the arts based on the theories of John Andrew Rice, who has had to leave his teaching post in a liberal arts college because of a "slight to the pre-established syllabus" (Katz, 2003, p 16). Rice attracts a like-minded group of educationalists from across the arts who are interested in exploring radical teaching methods and in managing themselves without a board of governors. Any "matters of grave importance" (p. 17) are to be discussed by the entire faculty and student body, although without a vote at the end. There are lectures and tutorials, but no credits or accreditation. Instead, students can request an exam when they feel ready. Faculty members are paid only bed and board as a sign of their commitment.

Rice puts the arts at the centre of the curriculum, and over time traditional subject boundaries dissolve as the focus of teaching is on process rather than content.

> Our central consistent effort is to teach method, not content; to emphasise process, to invite the student to the realisation that the way of handling facts is more important than the facts themselves. For facts change, while the method of handling facts... remains the same.
> (Katz, 2003, p. 28)

In terms of teaching, the emphasis is on integrating theory and practice and, as at the Bauhaus, on the primacy of materials – to shape the materials is to shape the world – along with the need for free experimentation so that students can find their own materials and styles.

At its best, BMC is characterized by is a strong sense of community, a "good-natured camp atmosphere" (Katz, 2003, p. 182), and an emphasis on group thinking and co-operative intelligence (p. 19). Art critic Juan Manuel Bonet sees BMC as like the Bauhaus but "more open and spontaneous", a "tremendous American adventure" which attracts a "fantastic and first-class" list of artists who are "central to modern culture (p. 11)." As for the students, artist Joseph Fiore testifies that "some people still say they felt free for the first time in their lives. They could do something on their own, not forced by anybody. It was a way of finding yourself" (p. 190).

Yet if BMC reproduces or even exceeds the triumphs of the Bauhaus in terms of its international reputation, it also reproduces the old dilemmas. As with the Bauhaus, without a strong organisational structure, the responsibility for holding the vision together, by any standards a complex and difficult task, rests with individual leaders. When in 1949 Albers leaves for Harvard, the college is vulnerable, "intellectually up for grabs" (Katz, 2003, p. 215). Albers' successor Charles Olson has neither the energy nor the imagination to hold the College together and by 1956 only four students remain in an atmosphere approaching anarchy as described by Michael Rumaker.

> There was a psychotic, unpredictable energy in the air. Jerry van de Wiele, the painter, told me that when certain students came to visit, when he was living at Last Chance on the road to the farm, he was careful to put the axe he used for cutting firewood in a safe place, out of sight and reach. (Katz, 2003, p. 216)

As Sir John Summerson will remind the Hornsey student rebels of 1969, "education… has to have some rigid parts to it. It's got to have an establishment, it's got to have a respectable lid on top of it…because I think it would fall apart, there has got to be some element of rigidity in it" (D.K. & V. H., 1969, p. 80).

6.3.5 The persistence paradox

A final paradox concerns the way in which the successive paradigms of Fine Art education seem to replace each other but at the same time persist in different contexts like private colleges, evening classes, or commercial art studios. Normally, as Kuhn points out, this wouldn't happen, as the point of new paradigms is to replace the old: "why dignify what science's best and most persistent efforts have made it possible to discard?" (Kuhn, [1962]1970, p. 138).

6.4 The historical narrative and the Framework of Educational Assumptions

If trying to understand Fine Art education in terms of a linear, historical narrative results in such a proliferation of problematics and paradoxes, what happens if we use the Framework of Educational Assumptions instead (Figure 3 below)?

6: INTERPRETING THE HISTORICAL NARRATIVE

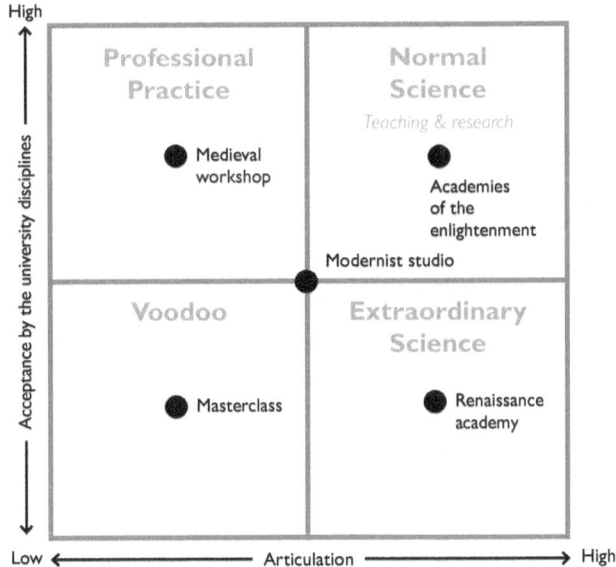

Figure 3. The historical narrative and the Framework of Educational Assumptions.

Here we can see how the paradigms identified by the historical narrative fit into different quadrants of the grid according to the social and intellectual preoccupations of the time. The narrative starts with the medieval workshop in the Professional Practice quadrant, with its emphasis on craft skills and apprenticeships. We then move towards Extraordinary Science in the Renaissance where the emphasis is on the exploration of new knowledge in informal, autonomous groups. In the enlightenment the focus moves to the Normal Science quadrant with its formal academies, followed by a retreat into the Voodoo quadrant with the Masterclass paradigm and the currency of ideas of genius. The narrative comes to rest in the centre of the grid in a position represented by the Bauhaus and the idea of the creative vacuum which accommodates aspects of all four quadrants.

Using the Framework in this way we can see the historical narrative as a shifting of emphasis between the quadrants, rather than as a linear progression which replaces one set of requirements with another as it moves forward.[31]

Rethinking the historical narrative in this way goes a long way to resolving the paradoxes and problematics noted above.

---

31 The sense that changes in art education are changes in emphasis rather than linear progressions is also present in de Duve's analysis (1994), although his interest is in movement along dimensions within the paradigm rather than across educational models.

The **progression paradox**, whereby developments in art education are talked about as both progressive and regressive, can be explained by the fact that moving around the grid is progressive in one way, since the new emphasis will give new perspective, but also regressive in others, since the change means de-emphasising something else which is still important.

The **pedagogical paradox**, whereby art is taught but cannot be taught, is resolved by seeing traditional teaching as only one element in the Framework, only relevant to the Normal Science quadrant and to a lesser extent Professional Practice. Activities relating to the quadrants Extraordinary Science and Voodoo are just as important for Fine Art education but since these are excluded from the university, they fall into the category of things which can't be taught.

The **performance paradox**, whereby successful students are not necessarily successful artists, is resolved by understanding how success is defined differently in each quadrant of the Framework. So in the Professional Practice quadrant success will be defined as technical merit, in the Normal Science quadrant as theoretical understanding, in the Extraordinary Science quadrant as the originality and conviction of the artist's vision, or in the Voodoo quadrant by freedom from any articulated norms. Achievement in one quadrant will not necessarily imply achievement in another, leaving the interesting question of who gets the prizes. Not surprisingly, the institution is more likely to give prizes which reflect the Normal Science or Professional Practice values with which it is familiar than for the more troubling Extraordinary Science or Voodoo values prized by the artists themselves.

The **relationship paradox,** whereby artists love and hate their institutions in equal measure, suggests that different students will have more or less affinity with different quadrants. So for example more conformist students will value the stability of the Normal Science and Professional Practice quadrants more than radical students who are more likely to value their experience of Extraordinary Science or Voodoo.

Similarly the **institutional paradox,** whereby the stronger the institution the less interesting it is, can be explained by the institution's natural identification with Normal Science and Professional Practice rather than with the autonomy of Extraordinary Science or the anarchy of Voodoo.

Finally, we can see that the **persistence paradox,** whereby apparently outmoded forms of art education nevertheless continue to exist, and Murakami's contemporary hi-tech art studio can "hark back to the time of Peter Paul Rubens" (Thornton, [2008]2009, p. 201), can be explained by recognising that while different aspects of art education may be emphasised by its institutions at particular times, they are displaced rather than replaced.

7 : Art and the university

'There is no doubt that studio art is marginalized in university life. But what exactly is the cure…I am engaged in finding ways to argue that fine art production has a place in the university. The problem is immensely difficult…'[32]

If we return now to where we left the historical narrative, we find that by the mid-twentieth century the elusive and paradoxical nature of art teaching and its institutions has resulted in a widespread sense of crisis. In America, art colleges have become a piecemeal collection of "private conservatories and schools of art" languishing in a state of economic and intellectual decline (Risenhoover & Blackburn, 1976, p. 3), while in the UK, art schools are characterised as failing institutions lacking in intellectual and pedagogical rigour.

For example, in 1923, the Camden Group painter Walter Sickert dismisses art students as "an immense mob of idlers, male and female, to whom art schools serve as a kind of day nursery" (Macdonald, 1973, p. 89). In the 1970s, architect and industrial designer Misha Black dismisses art colleges as "sanctuaries for the determined and refuges for the idle" (Black, 1973, p. 30); while art tutor Sjoerd Hannema at Manchester complains that:

> Generally speaking, the student is left to work out his own salvation…There are also those tutors, particularly common in the field of painting, who believe, as an article of faith, that students cannot and should not be taught; instead, they should be left to 'feel their way' and 'organize their own experience'. (Macdonald, 1973, p. 89)

In view of the institutional paradox noted in the previous chapter, this appearance of laissez-faire disarray may in fact be more productive than it appears, a version of the creative vacuum of the Bauhaus. But in the post-war world with its "new economic and social pressures" (Risenhoover & Blackburn, 1976, p. 5) and its emphasis on "relating costs to benefits in education" (Piper, 1973, p. 17), the elusive institutions of art education seem clearly "in crisis" with too many colleges, too many students, and not enough accountability. The solution is to draw "art education into the education mainstream": after centuries

---

32 Elkins, 2006, p. 246

of independence, the art academy is to become part of the "large conglomerate institutions" of the university system (p. 13). Or to use Risenhoover and Blackburn's folksy metaphor, a new settler is joining the natives (Risenhoover & Blackburn, 1976, p. 206).

7.1 The problem of integration

While the main point of the move to the universities is to resolve the organisational problems of the art schools, there remains the problem of how to integrate art's distinctive pedagogy. Like other educationalists of the time, David Warren Piper anticipates a period of mutual readjustment, with art tutors having "to argue their case to the scientists and technologists who seem to dominate the further education system" (Piper, 1973, p. 13).

> Some of the attitudes to learning, teaching procedures and language current in art education are often difficult for staff used to academic and technical teaching to understand and appreciate. Conversely the champions of the art schools often show an appalling ignorance of the rest of the education system. (Piper, 1973, p. 14)

In the US, Risenhoover and Blackburn (1976) anticipate that their research into "whether the university milieu provides a hospitable environment for an artist's professional activities" (p. ix) will uncover a "lack of congeniality between artists and universities", based on "divergences" which "conceivably could run deep".

> The university's is a verbal tradition whereas artists claim their creations are not reducible to words…it is thought that universities stultify, that their pure intellectualism distorts. As a bureaucracy they lack the necessary freedoms for the creative individual. So the critics say and so the artists wondered when they took their university positions.
> (Risenhoover & Blackburn, 1976, p. 11)

A certain amount of bias can be discerned in both accounts. Piper (1973, p. 14) characterises the art schools' independence as "an appalling ignorance" of the mainstream, while Risenhoover and Blackburn (1976) relegate the concept of irreducibility to the status of "claim", while associating intellectualism with the affirmative adjective "pure". Given this climate, it's hardly surprising that art teachers feared that their teaching would be compromised by the practices and values of mainstream pedagogy, with serious consequences for the kind of art students make. In the words of art critic Harold Rosenberg:

> Can there be any doubt that training in the university has contributed to the cool, impersonal wave in the art of the sixties? In the classroom – in contrast to the studio, which has tended to be dominated by metaphor – it is normal to formulate consciously what one is doing an to be able to explain it to others...creation is taken to be synonymous with productive processes. (Goldstein, 1996, p. 280).

Or as Thornton ([2008]2009) puts it, "there is a magic and an alchemy to art, but academics are always suspicious of the guy who stirs the big black pot" (p. 66).

7.2 Art as a discipline

At the operational level, the working solution to the problem of integration lies in the structure of academic disciplines. After all every discipline lays claim to its own special traditions and teaching practices, in the sciences as much as in the arts: "cellist and chemist may debate *means* from time to time (how better to finger a chord or remove an impurity from a sample), but their *ends* vary hardly at all" (Risenhoover & Blackburn, 1976, p. 201).

For Piper (1973), the "organisation of knowledge into subjects" (p. 24) is not only the basis of efficient teaching, but also the means of preserving the identity of different disciplines with their emphasis on different kinds of knowledge and appropriate teaching methods. In this respect, the discipline of art behaves in the same way as any other academic specialism.

> The subject exists as an entity... its standards of excellence are intrinsic to it, and...its qualities, of themselves, make it deserving of teaching. Fine Art would perhaps lend itself to this form of justification. (Piper, 1973, p. 24)

So Fine Art teaching can, perhaps, be black-boxed, packaged with "some old-style 'education'...book-reading, lectures, seminars, and so on" (T. N., 1969, p. 18), labelled as a discipline, and moved into the university framework with the minimum of disruption. The stirrers of the big black pot can continue their work uninterrupted.

In fact much of Risenhoover and Blackburn's (1976) study *Artists and Professors,* based on interviews with practising artists and musicians newly appointed to the American universities, seems to bear this out. In spite of initial concerns about integration from both sides, the authors discover that "for the most part, a happy union has taken place between artists and universities" (p. 12). Risenhoover and Blackburn's first interview is with Harold Altman, who has studied at the Bauhaus and Black Mountain College under Albers and now teaches at Pennsylvania State University. Altman's teaching seems unaffected by any newly acquired institutional requirements. He's able to work closely with individual students to develop their imagination and ideas in an atmosphere which provides "a kind of informality without the rigmarole and regulatory acts" (p. 22). He's always on the lookout for the student who shows independence and originality, who "doesn't look to the teacher for the stimulation, for the spoon-feeding" (p. 15). Altman admits to being accused of elitism (p. 27), and his frustrations with the university centre around the quality of students who are accepted: "you wouldn't expect Nadia Boulanger to take someone who is going to play chopsticks" (p. 30). He's also frustrated by the students' lack of engagement, partly as result of the academic demands made upon them (p. 29). But otherwise Altman seems philosophical about the demands of the university system: "I have learned…to be dishonest in a sense within the system…I've learned how to fight in situations" (pp. 24-26). He's certainly appreciative of the security it offers : "maybe I'm in a peaceable mood; I just had a great salary raise" (p. 19).

Goldstein's problematics rarely surface during these interviews, although in a curious exchange, artist Walter Kamys moves from talking about the excitement of teaching to reflecting on the performance paradox of art at the university, where tenure and a professorship are for an artist "…so fruitless, so hopeless…meaningless things in themselves" (Risenhoover & Blackburn, 1976, p. 91). The interviewer firstly ascribes this shift to Kamys' mood – "Have I caught you at a bad time? Are you down? Are you low today?" – before taking him to task for losing focus: "I think what I'm trying to tell you is that I don't understand where in the world we are" (p. 92). Kamys is quickly back on message.

> Sometimes I have egotistical faith in myself that I am a good teacher…I'll tell you one thing: I'm doing better work today than I have ever done in my entire life…I can go there when I'm feeling right, and I can do more in one hour today than I could in a week previously. (Risenhoover & Blackburn, 1976, p. 93)

Artist Rudy Pozzatti even claims to embrace institutional conflict as a necessary ingredient of the creative process: " …I think we all need some kind of agitation, disquieting influences…the difficult times are pretty damn important" (Risenhoover & Blackburn, 1976, p. 117).

From the evidence of these interviews, art tutors are managing the university system (and perhaps also their interviewers) by recognising its demands while at the same time preserving the integrity of their teaching. So Altman confesses that he does not "believe in grades anyway – total nonsense" (Risenhoover & Blackburn, 1976, p. 22), and that he actively discourages talentless students from continuing: "I try to turn him off; if he's wasting his time, I'm not going to waste my time..." (p. 23). Kamys subverts the university "factory" by prioritising the needs of his students over faculty demands (p. 93). Sculptor Jason Seley resists the pressure for visible performance by encouraging reflection over productivity: "I tend to think that the student is working when he is just thinking and being troubled and being puzzled...a lot of people don't feel that way" (p. 144).

This insulation of art from the university system, however, proves to be short-lived. As art historian Lisa Tickner observes, back in the UK a time-bomb has inadvertently been introduced into the black box which detonates in spectacular fashion at the Hornsey College of Art in 1968 (Tickner, 2008, p. 45).

7.3 The Hornsey revolution

The trigger for the events leading to the explosion of the time-bomb is Haringay's proposal to merge Hornsey College of Art with the Enfield and Hendon Colleges of Technology to form the new North London Polytechnic. According to Tickner (2008), in the violent clashes which follow the art students argue their case for autonomy with remarkable "fluency and verve", the result of a "satisfying historical irony" whereby the exposure of art students and staff to mainstream academic ways of thinking has unexpected consequences. Rather than leading them to conform to the system, as Rosenberg fears and Haringey probably hopes, staff and students instead discover a newfound confidence and articulacy which they bring to bear on a radical "debate on founding principles" (p. 47)

In Tickner's (2008) analysis, the agents of the revolution are the newly-recruited general studies staff brought in to add academic credibility to the art programme, "thrusting young academics, many of them left-leaning, imbued with university traditions of scepticism and free speech" who are charged, in Pevsner's words, with "occupying the intellect which does not get enough to bite on during studio hours and days" (Tickner, 2008, p. 47). T. N.'s (1969) account of his time at Hornsey as a social studies lecturer tells how he is struck by the gap between the College's international reputation as a "great bubbling hive of creativity and excitement" (p. 18) and the reality of the "mouldering school" where he holds seminars in a broom-cupboard with students who wait, more or less patiently, "for something to be done to them" (p. 19).

> How could the totally uncreative passivity of this medieval-schoolroom situation – which everyone obviously took for granted – give such heady fruits? The contradiction made one's mind reel. (T. N., 1969, p. 19).

T.N.'s teaching takes place separately from the traditional art-school teaching of the "old studio blue-bloods" (T. N., 1969, p. 18), but by "stirring up the minds of the students…provoking a modicum of self-activity" (p. 19), the fix is in. Although the students lose the fight for autonomy at Hornsey, "history is not always written by the victors or even kind to them". The legacy of Hornsey is the appropriation of academic forms of analysis by artists to re-examine fundamental questions about "what art is or can be for, the role of design…[and]…the best means of educating students in either or both", which are "still questions for us now" (Tickner, 2008, p. 102). As Elkins observes, "by adopting the language of the social sciences, art education enables itself to ask and answer different kinds of questions" (2001, p. 41).

7.4 Analysing Fine Art

McGilchrist (2009) characterises the "enormous strength" of the left hemisphere of the brain, which is responsible for rational analysis, as its ability to "unfold, or unpack, what it is given" (p. 208). So the appropriation of academic forms of analysis by art as a discipline results in new ways of exploring the issues associated with art teaching.

For example, Thierry de Duve's essay *When form has become attitude – and beyond* (de Duve, 1994), is, according to Tickner (2008), "an article of incisive brilliance" (p. 90) for the way in which it provides a framework for classifying different kinds of art education. De Duve proposes a series of shifting dimensions: talent versus creativity (de Duve, 1994, p. 27), métier versus medium (p. 28), imitation versus invention (p. 30), talent and creativity versus attitude (p. 33), metier and medium versus practice (p. 35), and imitation and invention versus deconstruction (p. 36). According to this analysis, the various paradigms of art education can be identified as tripartite structures which combine differently at different times. For example in the early academies the combination is of talent–métier–imitation, changing to the combination of creativity–medium–invention in the twentieth century, and to the current combination of attitude–practice–deconstruction. De Duve's analysis provides for the first time a theoretical model of the dimensions of art teaching, in contrast to the descriptive historical narratives of Pevsner (1940) and Goldstein (1996). Although de Duve is aware that the reality of art schools is "a lot more complex, more subtle, and more ambiguous" (Tickner, 2008, p. 90) than his model may imply, it nevertheless represents an important step beyond description and towards explanation.

Elkins' *Why art cannot be taught* (2001) also applies the analytical approach with a view to "providing ways for teachers and students to make sense of the experience of learning art". In his chapter on critiques (p. 111), for example, Elkins suggests five ways of classifying critiques ("amorous, linguistic, narratological, warlike, and legal" (p. 147)) and two ways of classifying the kinds of comments tutors make ("judicative and descriptive" (p. 150)). Elkins is aware that this approach only works for the "few moments that are susceptible to analysis" (p. 95), and that the analysis itself will have no direct relationship with better teaching (p. 109), but he still believes it's important. Only by being explicit about their work can art tutors reach some sort of consensus about what they do, and, ultimately, how to improve it. Without this understanding "it does not make sense to propose fundamental curricular changes in the ways art is taught" (p. 109), since any change could equally be for better or for worse.

7.5 Experimental paradigms

The new insights resulting from appropriating academic analysis result in a series of radical proposals about how art should be taught at the university. While the wholesale curriculum changes proposed by the Hornsey students are rejected, a series of radical experiments do find a place in the university system, perhaps because it's "easier to plan a radical course than a whole new institution" (Tickner, 2008, p. 94). These experimental paradigms are described below.

7.5.1 The geodesic dome or network

The paradigm of the geodesic dome[33] or network comes from the Hornsey students' alternative proposal to the traditional linear system of education. In this paradigm the art studio is a project space leading to any number or type of related "areas of skill and knowledge" (Tickner, 2008, p. 51), in a way which is both flexible and structured at the same time, like a geodesic dome. The class group is "an important source of motivation and support" (p. 50), but in reality each student must construct their own journey in a way which correlates "skills and disciplines in relation to the aims of particular projects" (p. 50). The tutor's role

- - - - -

33 The name of the paradigm reflects the influence of Buckminster Fuller, one-time teacher at Black Mountain College and creator of the geodesic dome, who comes out in support of the Hornsey students.

is to ensure that students define their project objectives clearly in a way which prevent the students' work from descending into an "anarchic bogey" of form or content (pp. 51-52).

At their *Hornsey strikes again* exhibition at the Institute of Contemporary Arts, the Hornsey students prepare a "didactic demonstration" of the benefits of such a network system over the constraints of the proposed Diploma in Art and Design (DipAD). Visitors are led down the DipAD route consisting of dimly-lit, narrow corridors, with taped voices firing intimidating questions about qualifications and "tedious questions on the history of art" (Tickner, 2008, p. 57). Visitors finally emerge into an open area surrounded by multi-screen projected images, where they are invited to take part in free discussion and argument in an open atmosphere which is the antithesis of the narrow constraints of the DipAD. In any pragmatic curriculum sense, this paradigm is, according to Tickner, "a kind of fantasy" (p. 51). For the students, however, the proof of its effectiveness is in the way in which the sit-in is organised.

> We are demonstrating that it is entirely possible for a body of students to take over and properly organize, in co-operation with our tutors, a curriculum in which individual needs are no longer subordinated to a predetermined system of training requiring a degree of specialization which precludes the broad development of the student's artistic and intellectual capabilities. (D. P., 1969, p. 56)

With which Tickner agrees: "the sit-in at its best was an exemplary educational experience" (2008, p. 72).

7.5.2 The white room

In the late 1960's, sculptor Peter Kardia at St Martins School of Art follows his intuition that habit is the greatest threat to creativity by devising a studio programme to deliberately disorientate students and force them to new insights. For their first term, new students are locked in a white studio for eight hours a day for an unspecified number of weeks with only one kind of material. Without instructions and forbidden to speak to each other, they are deliberately put in a position where they can have no way of rationalising what they are doing (Tickner, 2008, p. 95). The studio is defined as a space free from conventional constraints, where students must discover for themselves a new, individual orientation.

7.5.3 The art theory paradigm

In 1969, in their Art Theory course at Coventry, tutors Terry Atkinson, Michael Baldwin, and David Bainbridge argue that traditional assumptions about the nature and practice of art fatally compromise the work of art students. So art teaching should offer a "deconstructive critique" of the givens of art such as "the primacy of the art-object, the importance of formal experiment in the medium, and the creative autonomy of artists and students" (Tickner, 2008, p. 96). The emphasis is on language, with "fiercely articulate tutors" (p. 97) dismantling students' preconceptions. The programme is short-lived, since only tangible art objects qualify for assessment at the university. However it provides an interesting marker for where the boundaries of studio teaching at the university might lie.

7.5.4 The consciousness-raising paradigm

Artist Judy Chicago's 1970/71 course at Fresno State College in the US focuses on the issues of women as artists. Chicago believes that role conditioning and socialisation prevent women from reaching their potential in a male-dominated profession where they are asked to work on projects that have little to do with their own lives and concerns. Chicago's group meets outside college, going to the theatre, cinema, and concerts together at the same time as developing their own critique "of the values and institutions of mainstream modernism", before returning to the studio to " stop talking and start preparing art" (Tickner, 2008, p. 97). Chicago's paradigm is radical in the attention it pays to the role of personal experience and self-expression in students' work.

7.5.5 The performance paradigm

In this paradigm, the art tutor orchestrates the studio critique as a performance, integrating student work with their peers' responses to form an immersive experience. An example of this paradigm is provided by Thornton ([2008]2009, pp. 43-73) in her description of the "legendary" crit class conducted by Michael Asher at CalArts. Asher has been running this class since 1974, during which time it has gained a formidable reputation as a "once-in-a-lifetime experience", with a number of artists of international repute describing it as "one of the most memorable and formative experiences of their art education" (p. 45).

Asher directs the performance: Thornton is allowed to attend only if she is silent, since she may disturb the chemistry of the class. Indeed the unpromising "airless institutional space" where the crit is to take place immediately reminds Thornton of "an Asher installation", typified by dynamic, ephemeral qualities (Thornton, [2008]2009, p. 44).

The crit centres on the work of three students who, in addition to their work, bring along snacks as "an acknowledged peace offering to their peers" (Thornton, [2008]2009, p. 45). The student audience arrives with laptops, sleeping bags, pillows and even dogs, who are allowed as long as they are quiet, and who are perceived as contributors since "dogs are emotional sponges. They're attuned to the mood" (pp. 46-47).

As the crit begins with student Josh introducing his work,"two large, well-crafted pencil drawings" (Thornton, [2008]2009, p. 47), audience members define their territory through "a pet, a pose, or a signature activity" such as life drawing, knitting or quilting (p. 48). As newcomers arrive they too contribute to the activity in the room by eating, drinking, writing emails, and passing notes to each other. Asher's only articulated rule is that "students have to listen to and respect each other" but as Thornton observes, "a chimp could sense the enduring layers of convention" in the room (p. 49). Everyone has their role to play: this is not an event for the uninitiated.

Over four hours pass in a "very abstract and often inchoate ongoing debate" (Thornton, [2008]2009, p.51) with a minimum of intervention from Asher, for whom it is important that the students set their own agenda: the students describe his style as "minimal and abstract" (p. 56). After an hour's break the crit resumes with student Fiona presenting her work, and by eight o'clock in the evening the conversation is "spiraling amorphously" around exhausted students and sleeping dogs. Pizzas are ordered in as more students (and dogs) join for the evening session when the final student Hobbs presents his work. As the evening progresses, many students fall in and out of sleep until at one in the morning the "epic" crit finally comes to an end and Asher takes his leave (p. 70).

For Thornton, the experience has transformed the teaching space from "dry and institutional" to something "complicated and inspired". Asher's crit is a "minimalist performance where the artist has sat, listened with care, and occasionally cleared his throat" (Thornton, [2008]2009, p. 73). She notices that the word IRAQ has been added to the exit sign, which seems a significant metaphor: "the space is no longer a banal box but a war-torn landscape" (p. 71) where intellectual territory has been strenuously contested.

7.6 Experimental paradigms and the Framework of Educational Assumptions

Figure 4 below shows the results of mapping these experimental paradigms onto the Framework of Educational Assumptions.

7: ART AND THE UNIVERSITY

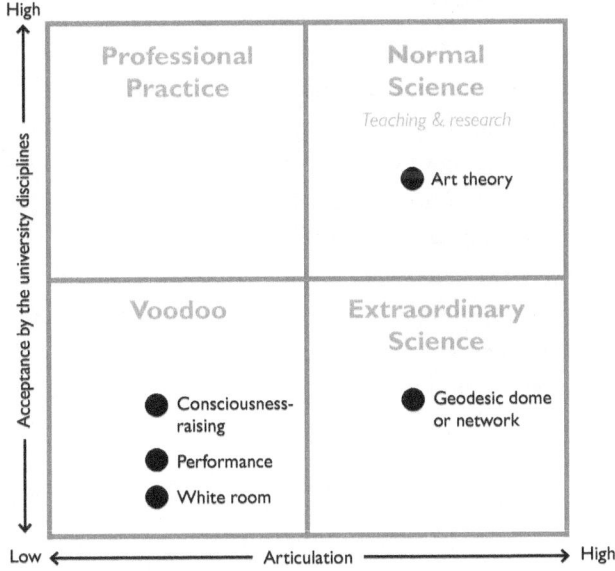

Figure 4. Experimental paradigms and the Framework of Educational Assumptions.

In the **geodesic dome** paradigm, the teaching environment is both structured and flexible. The role of the teacher is to support students as they develop their individual learning paths. This emphasis on creating new knowledge from existing structures puts it in the Extraordinary Science quadrant.

The **art-theory** experiment entirely removes the element of the making of artworks from the studio in favour of discussion and analysis. This positions art theory in the Normal Science quadrant.

The remaining experimental paradigms emphasise the personal, unarticulated dimensions of art teaching, perhaps as an antidote to the intellectualising tendencies of the university. There is certainly something of the Voodoo about Kardia's white room experiment where all cognitive references are removed in the interests of self-discovery, or in Asher's teaching as performance where the immersive experience results in distortions of time, space, and meaning. Meanwhile in Judy Chicago's consciousness-raising experiment the emphasis is on emotional awareness and self-belief as much as the production of art.

7.7 Who's influencing whom?

If bringing art into the universities introduces art teachers to new ways of analysis and thinking about their work, has this been reciprocal? Is there evidence of art teaching influencing the university in its turn?

We have seen how, using the analogy of new settlers arriving in territories already occupied by "old-timers", Risenhoover and Blackburn (1976, p. 212) anticipate that the introduction of the discipline of Fine Art will have a significant impact on the universities. Art teachers "can teach the university about creativity and productivity…highly important matters regarding the creative side" (p. 213). They are likely to be attuned to more subjective criteria for excellence than their science colleagues (p. 206), and to be instrumental in establishing the conditions for "sparking innovations", given their propensity to "try something new for the fun of it" (p. 208).

At the Hornsey sit-in, however, D. K. and V. H. are more sceptical. For them, the relationship between Fine Art and the university is one-sided. Art students are required to augment their studio practice with academic studies in the interests of a balanced education. However the same can't be said for students of academic subjects who by the same logic should practise art for a similar proportion of their time.

> The introduction of Liberal Studies to art colleges would have made sense if 20 per cent of a college degree course had been devised in free expression, from which many university students would surely have benefited. (D. K. and V. H., 1969, p. 86)

Macleod and Holdridge's experiences of negotiating for the acceptance of art PhDs is another indicator of this one-sided relationship, showing the university's very real difficulties in recognising the validity of art as a discipline, let alone adopting its methods.

> Much is said about artists' ignorance, their lack of ability to write academic texts, to undertake comprehensive surveys of research terrain and to appropriately undertake research. (Macleod & Holdridge, 2006, p. 7)

The reasons for this asymmetrical relationship are undoubtedly complex, but McGilchrist's (2009) work on the divided brain may provide one source of explanation. If we take the split between right- and left-brained ways of thinking as a metaphor for the arts/science divide, it seems that the inherent flexibility of the right brain will be open to the influence of the left brain, but that the left brain cannot reciprocate.

> The more flexible style of the right hemisphere is evidenced not just in its own preferences, but also at the 'meta' level, in the fact that it can also use the left hemisphere's preferred style, whereas the left hemisphere cannot use the right hemisphere's. (McGilchrist, 2009, p. 41)

This suggests that while art is intrinsically open to new experience, the university will be strongly defended against it. If art teaching is to become part of the university culture as a whole and influence how science is taught, it needs to be able to adapt to the preferred style of the left hemisphere and of the university: it needs to be explained.

Part 3:
Fieldwork

8: The role of discourse analysis

'What I am attempting to bring to light is the epistemological field, the episteme in which knowledge, envisaged apart from all criteria having reference to its rational value or to its objective forms, grounds its positivity, and thereby manifests a history which is not that of its growing perfection, but rather that of its conditions of possibility.'[34]

Up until now we've been thinking about Fine Art paradigms in terms of their theory and history. This has given us a good sense of how Fine Art differs from other disciplines insofar as it recognizes kinds of knowledge (Voodoo and Extraordinary Science) which are excluded from the university with its focus on Normal Science and Professional Practice.

Moving from history to the present day, the question now is about where contemporary Fine Art fits on the Framework. Surprisingly, in spite of the huge social, economic and intellectual transitions since the Bauhaus, it seems that no significantly new or enduring paradigm has emerged during this period. De Duve (1994, p. 26) sees the contemporary art curriculum as "obsolete" and "in open crisis", while Elkins (2001) seems in a constant state of exasperation about the complacency and mediocrity of both the education art students receive and the artworks they produce.

We need to find a way to look more closely at the contemporary paradigm, at what's happening now in the art departments of universities. And to do this, we need a research method which will resist the invisible boundaries of paradigms and give us insights into the things we can't easily see: we need discourse analysis.

The rest of this chapter looks at the theory and practice of discourse analysis as a background to the fieldwork presented in Chapters 9, 10 and 11.

8.1 Foucault and the theory of discourse analysis

Our starting point for the theory of discourse analysis is with French philosopher Michel Foucault, whose theoretical texts, *The Order of Things* ([1966]2012)

---
34 Foucault, [1966]2012, p. xxv

and *The Archaeology of Knowledge* ([1969]2002]), set out the principles and the insights which inform its practice.

The idea most associated with Foucault, and to which he returns repeatedly, is that all discourse is informed by an archaeological level of knowledge, invisible, implied, and hidden below the surface[35]. By way of illustration, Foucault's introduction to *The Order of Things* ([1966]2012) famously presents us with a passage of text from Borges purporting to come from a Chinese encyclopaedia. This passage classifies animals by means of an unexpected taxonomy:

"(a) belonging to the Emperor, (b) embalmed, (c) tame, (d) sucking pigs, (e) sirens, (f) fabulous, (g) stray dogs, (h) included in the present classification, (i) frenzied, (j) innumerable, (k) drawn with a very fine camelhair brush, (l) *et cetera*, (m) having just broken the water pitcher, (n) that from a long way off look like flies." Foucault, [1966]2012, p. xvi

To accept this taxonomy would "break up all the ordered surfaces and all the planes with which we are accustomed to tame the wild profusion of existing things" (p. xvi). While each element makes sense in itself, putting them together confronts us with "the stark impossibility of thinking *that*" within our existing systems of thought (p. xvi). We can find no common ground for bringing these elements together: no "table", "hidden network", "grid", "inner law" (p. xxi) or "hidden order" (p. xxii) to make this particular discourse possible. From this example we can see that, if we are to view our world at all coherently, there must be a level of shared knowledge and assumptions beneath the surface of our discourse (p. xxiv).

Foucault provides a number of historical examples of how underlying beliefs constrain the discourse of particular periods. For example, we tend to think of sixteenth century learning as "an unstable mixture" (Foucault, [1966]2012, p. 35) of rational knowledge, magical belief, and classical cultural references. In fact, however, these distinctions are impossible for sixteenth century thinkers who believe, at the archaeological level, that the world is "covered with signs that must be deciphered" and for whom "divination is not a rival form of knowledge; it is part of the main body of knowledge itself" (p. 36). Another of Foucault's examples comes from the seventeenth century, when linear, rationalist definitions of knowledge lead to an increasing emphasis on the precise definitions of words and the rules of grammar. In this period, the choice and

---

35 Foucault's archaeological metaphor compares with Hudson's ([1972]1974) metaphor of the paradigm as a dark undercurrent. Foucault's metaphor is from the objective historian's perspective, while Hudson's reflects his personal intellectual history. Both agree, however, on the force of what lies below the surface.

arrangement of words are not simply matters of aesthetics or function but a precise representation of knowledge itself: "…language is an analysis of thought: not a simple patterning, but a profound establishment of order in space" (p. 91). Foucault cites Diderot who tells us that "the language of a people gives us its vocabulary, and its vocabulary is a sufficiently faithful and authoritative record of all the knowledge of that people" (p. 97). In this context, mistakes in language or grammar are mistakes in thinking, which need to be put right.[36]

Foucault acknowledges the resonance of the idea of an archaeological level of knowledge with structuralist paradigms, but his intention is at once broader and more subtle. While structuralists set out to uncover, describe, and analyse the big ideas that inform our social history, Foucault is less interested in "all those themes whose function is to ensure the infinite continuity of discourse" (Foucault, [1969]2002, p. 28) than in "the living, fragile, pulsating" history, (p. 12) revealed by a particular discourse at a particular point in time. His perspective is vertical rather than horizontal, a snapshot through all the systems of dependencies (p. 81) invoked by a particular discourse as opposed to the horizontal or historical tracing of themes through time.

Foucault is careful to emphasise that his interest in the invisible dimensions of discourse is not at the expense of its explicit meanings at the surface level, the "existing unities" ([1969]2002, p. 79) of finished discourse. Understanding the assumptions which make a particular discourse possible is merely an elaboration of its explicit meaning, an extension of what can be seen. Foucault considers making a distinction between the underlying systems and the "visible façade" of language by calling the former *prediscursive*, but decides that the distinction is ultimately unnecessary since each level implies the other, and both together make up what we understand by discourse (p. 84).

8.1.1 Definitions

Foucault defines discourse thematically, where "statements different in form, and dispersed in time, form a group if they refer to one and the same object" (Foucault, [1969]2002, p. 34). In his own work, the themes of madness and mental illness define a discourse which crosses the boundaries of both time and subject matter and includes the disciplines of science, medicine, philosophy, and social policy (p. 35). In academic terms, themes transcend disciplines: "could one not, for example, constitute as a unity everything that has constituted the evolutionist theme from Buffon to Darwin?" (p. 39).

---

36 This legacy may explain the fervour of grammarians today, who are apt to associate failures of punctuation particularly among young people with cracks in the structure of society.

Foucault also considers how best to define the fundamental unit of discourse. Obvious choices from a range of disciplines would be the sentence, the proposition, or the speech act (Foucault, [1969]2002, pp. 90-91), but these tend to focus on the surface characteristics of language. Foucault opts instead for the *statement* (p. 98). The statement is any "series of signs, figures, marks or traces" (p. 95) that creates meaning. Statements have four necessary attributes:

- They have meaning in the sense of referring to something that we recognise – they "cannot be non-significant" (p. 102)

- Their subject is both the author and the discourse community the author represents (p. 104)

- They are related to a particular field or domain (p. 199)

- They have a material existence (p. 118).

8.1.2 Methods

Foucault acknowledges the difficulty of finding ways to achieve "the systematic description of a discourse-object" (Foucault, [1969]2002, p. 156) in its full contextual complexity. How do we define the boundaries of a particular discourse? What kind of sampling is it safe to adopt? What level of analysis is appropriate, in terms of both content and grammatical form? What methods of analysis should we use? (pp. 11-12). In the light of uncertainties such as these, Foucault's claims to any kind of a definitive methodology are tentative, and his proposals are presented in a "cautious, stumbling manner" (p. 18).

Foucault is emphatic, however, about what suitable methods will not be. They will not constitute any formal orthodoxy of which he believes there are more than enough already (Foucault [1969]2002, p. 152). Neither will they be concerned with the conventional histories of big ideas as represented in the disciplines, or with revealing general forms (p. 175).

Foucault imagines the methods of discourse analysis as a series of concentric circles (Foucault, [1969]2002, p. 128) with the main theme of the discourse at the centre and the more "enigmatic" possibilities such as the politics (p. 136) and the histories (pp. 142-148) relating to it on the outside. Discourse analysts traverse these circles at will in order to make the full context of the discourse "visible and analysable" (p. 126) and disclose as much of its meaning as possible.

We've seen that Foucault sees the discourse associated with a particular theme as going beyond the boundaries of any single academic discipline. So specialist, single-discipline methods of analysis won't be enough

(Foucault, [1966]2012, p. xiv). In fact, Foucault sees no direct connection at all between his approach to discourse and the approach taken by other disciplines:[37] "archaeology does not describe disciplines" ([1969]2002], p. 197). By way of illustration, he takes the example of analysing a painting (p. 213). A discipline-based approach will look for what he calls the "latent discourse" of the painting. This might include the artist's intentions in using particular lines, surfaces, and colours; the implicit philosophy behind the painting; or the science or opinions of the period it reflects (p. 214). What Foucault wants to know, however, is none of these things. Taking the picture as "a discursive practice embodied in techniques and effects" (p. 206) he's interested in the context of its formation, what's being said and taught about painting at that time, and why it's this painting and no other.

As an alternative to discipline-based approaches, Foucault argues for comparative methods which put disciplines side by side either with other disciplines or with different versions of themselves, in a way which enables us to see past traditional boundaries to either common ideological sources (Foucault, [1966]2012, p. xiv) or "points of incompatibility" (Foucault, [1969]2002]), p. 73). This is the approach adopted in *The Order of Things* ([1966] 2012). Here Foucault chooses three different disciplines around which to focus his inquiry: grammar, natural history, and economics (p. xv). Of course this choice can be seen as arbitrary, personal, and idiosyncratic. But the identity of the disciplines he chooses is actually irrelevant: the act of comparison is what counts, as it reveals hidden boundaries. Disciplines are substitutable, and others could work equally well.

As an example of how comparative methods work, Foucault makes a comparison between Aldrovandi's natural history *A History of Serpents and Dragons* and Jonston's *Natural History of Quadrupeds*, written half a century later in 1657 (Foucault, [1966]2012, p. 141). Both men, he judges, know about as much as each other about the animals they describe. But while Aldrovani includes all kinds of evidence including "a description of its anatomy and of the methods of capturing it; its allegorical uses and mode of generation; its habitat and legendary mansions; its food and the best way of cooking its flesh", Jonston gives us only information under 12 analytical headings. The comparative analysis shows that "the essential difference lies in what is *missing* in Jonston". This is not because Aldrovani is particularly naïve, but because he makes different

---

37 Foucault takes disciplines to be "groups of statements that borrow their organization from scientific models, which tend to coherence and demonstrativity" (p. 197).

assumptions about knowledge and the nature of the represented world which only become visible by comparison with Jonston.

Comparative methods let us see one discourse "in a relation of analogy, opposition, or complementarity with certain other discourses" (Foucault, [1969]2002]), p. 74). Statements which appear in different contexts can still be seen as similar (p. 73) either because they're formed in the same way or because they follow the same rules. Insights can come from comparing one form of language with another, often across traditional divides of time or discipline. Discourse analysis is interested in both unity and diversity (p. 177), where the rules apply and where they're broken (p. 178), the discourse and the social context surrounding it (p. 178), and changes over time (p. 187). Its aim is "not to overcome differences but to analyse them, to say what they consist of and to differentiate them" (p. 189).

An obvious starting point for making comparisons like this is to identify the rules that apply to a particular discourse, in order to answer the question, "according to what rules has a particular statement been made, and consequently according to what rules could other similar statements be made?" (Foucault, [1969]2002, p. 30). The idea is not to provide an exhaustive analysis of the intellectual systems which have produced the discourse (p. 66), but to look for patterns and recurrences in the ways in which ideas either cohere or exclude each other (p. 67). These are the distinctive "intrinsic regularities" (p. 69) or rules of a given discourse which operate independently of individual speakers and which will reveal the conceptual field (p. 70).

For Foucault, the uniqueness of any given statement can result from a practically inexhaustible list of reasons, many of which will be evident from their "surfaces of emergence" in the discourse in question (p. 45). These might include:

- The connection of the words to the gesture of writing or of speech
- The relationship with remembered statements
- The materiality of the form of the statement
- The fact that it may be subject to "repetition, transformation, and reactivation" in the future
- Its relationship with what comes before and after it.

Other reasons might be related to genre, for example the "degrees of rationalization, conceptual codes, and types of theory" in scientific or academic discourse ([1969]2002, p. 45).

Rules are also at work in the structure of the text and the way in which it's organised. For example scientific writing uses the structure of setting up a hypothesis and then proving it (the hypothesis/verification dependency) (Foucault, [1969]2002, p. 63). "Fields of presence" are the rules about which ideas are accepted and which excluded (p. 64). "Fields of concomitance" are the rules which determine the relationships of ideas with each other (p. 64), and "procedures of intervention" (p. 65) refer to how the discourse gets to its present form through a process of editing and transcribing (p. 65).

If we can work out the rules of a given discourse, we can start to see both how they shape it and when there are deviations. This will lead to insights beyond the kind of easy assumptions about genre or category which Foucault sees as mere "hasty unities or syntheses" (Foucault, [1969]2002, p. 33). The more we research the regularities of different discourses and the hidden rules or hierarchies within them, the more we'll understand the forces invoked by even "the least statement – the most discreet or the most banal" (p. 163).

As well as understanding the rules, we also need to understand who are the "authorities of delimitation" (Foucault, [1969]2002) responsible for both the rules and the systems and classifications assumed by the discourse. We also need to understand the status and authority of the person who's speaking and of the organisation they represent (p. 56).

Finally, we need to be alert to the various roles speakers adopt at different times in a given discourse. For example, a doctor can be variously "the sovereign, direct questioner, the observing eye, the touching finger, the organ that deciphers signs, the point at which previously formulated descriptions are integrated, the laboratory technician" (Foucault, [1969]2002, p. 58) and adopt a different form of discourse for each role.

Foucault distinguishes his interest in language from that of traditional linguists whose concern is with the mechanics of language (Foucault, [1969]2002, p. 121). While there is value in this kind of investigation, discourse analysis has to look beyond grammar or surface structure or the "things said" to what is hidden and unsaid, the "exclusions, limits, or gaps" (p. 122) that situate the discourse.

In his conclusion to *The Archaeology of Knowledge* ([1969]2002), Foucault acknowledges the practical challenges raised by his concept of discourse analysis, governed as it is by "an obscure set of anonymous rules" (p. 231). He also recognises the emotional challenges that go with acknowledging that our discourse is a "complex, differentiated practice governed by analysable rules and transformations" as much as the unique reflection of "what [we] think, believe and imagine" (p. 232).

8.2 Discourse analysis in practice

Following Foucault, the field of discourse analysis has been mostly concerned with developing consistent and reliable ways of putting Foucault's ideas into practice.

8.2.1 Definitions and disciplines

Foucault's decision to define discourse thematically is further developed in Etienne Wenger's ([1998]2005) work on communities of practice. Wenger sees "styles and discourses" (p. 129) as the materials from which local communities create their own histories and identities. He extends the definition of *discourse* to include not only written texts but also speech acts, leading to our current understanding of discourse as "socially-situated language-use in any channel or medium", even including "sign languages of the deaf...textual graphics...and images" (Cameron, [2001]2006, p. 7).

In theory, as we have seen, defining discourse thematically should make discourse analysis a cross-disciplinary activity. In practice however discipline boundaries are not so easy to ignore and discourse analysis seems to have been appropriated by a number of interested disciplines and construed in their own terms. "Anthropologists, linguists, philosophers, psychologists, sociologists, students of the media or education or the law" (Cameron, [2001]2006), p. 7) are all contenders, each with their own interests and areas of expertise. Cameron (pp. 47-52) provides us with an overview of each discipline's approach:

- Anthropology is interested in what discourse reveals about the culture of a society in relation to other societies
- Philosophy is concerned with how meaning is produced through language
- Sociology looks at the role of discourse in the construction of social order
- Linguistics looks at the structure of language and the distribution of linguistic forms
- Sociolinguistics shows how utterances are put together in logical sequences
- Critical discourse analysis considers the ideological choices behind what speakers chose to say or not say.

In the light of such diversity, it's hardly surprising that Stubbs ([1983]1995, p. 1) concludes that "the term *discourse analysis* is very ambiguous".

On the whole the most natural home for discourse analysis seems to be linguistics, including both applied linguistics and sociolinguistics.[38] For Stubbs ([1983]1995, p. 12) the reality is that while "the subject is at once too vast, and too lacking in focus and consensus" to be comprehensively defined, the insights of linguistics are at least no more partial and controversial than those of any other discipline. While he maintains that "I do not wish to argue…that linguistics *is* discourse analysis" (p. 219), he nevertheless implies a close identification.

8.2.2 Tools and techniques

So it's to various branches of linguistics that we can look to find the tools and techniques of discourse analysis practice. Because of their origin, these tools tend to focus on the mechanics of language and the patterns and structures of discourse rather than the contexts in which it takes place and the meanings it produces.

These tools also enable some remarkably detailed textual analysis. In particular linguist Harvey Sacks' *conversation analysis* is associated with scrupulous attention to the details of spoken discourse. Sacks is interested in providing a "rigorous, empirical and formal way" of understanding the structure and organisation of what's being said (Coulthard, [1977]1985, p. 59), which involves collecting all kinds of data – for example paralinguistic (intonation and accent), kinesic (body motion), and proxemic (body position) – as well as spoken interactions and the silences between words. This approach results in a richness of data leading to legendary interpretation times. Stubbs ([1983]1995, p. 222) tells how Sacks famously spent a year interpreting one piece of data (although presumably not exclusively), and how Pittenger et al. took 25-30 hours to transcribe five minutes of a psychiatric interview. Cameron ([2001]2006, p. 739) tells of experienced researchers who take a whole day to transcribe a few minutes of spoken discourse. Ultimately, though, the microscopic approach is not always helpful. It may help us to see the object clearly, but has nothing to say about what we are looking at (Stubbs, [1983]1995, p. 238).

In reality, given the complexity of spoken discourse, and the fact that "we must accept that a speaker can do anything he likes at any time" (Coulthard, [1977]1985, p. 145), it's unrealistic to expect a clear set of rules for discourse analysis (Stubbs, [1983]1995, p. 219). Answering the questions raised by

---

38 Applied linguistics is interested in real-life language problems rather than constructed language examples; sociolinguistics looks at language variation in relation to, for example, ethnicity, gender, religion, and power.

Foucault (identifying the boundaries of the discourse, sampling, levels of analysis, and types of analyses), inevitably involves making judgements based on the aims of the research. Cameron's ([2001]2006) insight is helpful here when she observes that "there is…a distinction to be made between analysing discourse as an end in itself and analysing it as a means to some other end" (p. 7).[39] Linguistically-oriented studies whose interest is in how people talk will naturally put a greater emphasis on detailed descriptions of the mechanics of the discourse, compared with studies using discourse analysis as a means to an end. These will be more selective and concentrate only on methods that will produce relevant data. For example, an anthropologist may collect large quantities of discourse data over a period of years (p. 54), in contrast to a sociolinguist who may focus on a mere "fragment of conversation" as a basis for the development of a particular theory (Stubbs, ([1983]1995, p. 220).

Just because there's no one way to go about discourse analysis, however, doesn't mean that anything goes. Early studies of discourse are often criticised for being too casual in their approach to the integrity of the text or too subjective in its interpretation, relying on judgement rather than any objective measures (Stubbs [1983]1995, pp. 228-9). Whatever their purpose, discourse analysis approaches need to be designed systematically and to make use of accepted tools and techniques, since:

> There is no going back on the standards of explanation and rigour set by the kind of structural linguistics created principally by Saussure, Bloomfield and Chomsky. However it has become increasingly clear that a coherent view of language, including syntax, must take account of discourse phenomena. (Stubbs, [1983]1995, pp. 6-7)

Tools and techniques can enable both structural and thematic analysis.

Structural analysis is based on the understanding that the structure of discourse contributes as much to its meaning as the literal sense of the words (Stubbs [1983]1995, p. 84). Irrespective of content, the structural frame predicts the nature of the discourse (p. 97). It sets limits in advance on what can be said, the way in which it's said (p. 84), and by whom. Stubbs uses the example of a phone call he makes to a college to verify the address of a colleague. When he asks the receptionist, "Does X works here?" she responds by putting his call through, since this is what the question invariably implies (p. 98). Here

---

39 Coulthard ([1977]1985) makes a similar point when he talks about the two approaches to discourse analysis, "one concerned with sequential relationships, the other with interpretation; the one working for 'rules'…the other for 'procedure'" (p. viii).

structural expectations override the literal meaning of the question "Does X works here?" to which the logical answer is "yes" or "no".

In spite of, or because of, our familiarity with the structural rules that govern our discourse, intuitive judgements about them are "notoriously unreliable" (Stubbs [1983]1995, p. 129) whether they are made by observers or participants. The tools and techniques of structural analysis are designed to give us objective data which is consistent and manageable, resisting the complexity of the discourse and its theoretically limitless potential for classification (p. 61). Structural analysis looks at patterns such as:

- Patterns of dominance based on the proportion of the discourse for which each speaker is responsible
- Patterns of exchange such as the average length of exchanges, who initiates the exchange and who ends it
- Patterns of participation showing who talks to whom
- The use of meta-communication to frame the discourse
  (Stubbs; Coulthard ([1977]1985); Cameron ([2001]2006).

Thematic analysis is concerned with the content of the discourse, both explicit and implicit. Like structural analysis, it looks for patterns within the text, their content, frequency, and inter-relationship. An important principle of thematic analysis is that the themes are derived from the data rather than the intentions of the participants and what people think they are saying. This is particularly relevant in formal contexts such as teaching, where what teachers say they are doing may lead us to make assumptions about the subject of the discourse which aren't verified by the text.

8.3 Educational discourse

We've seen from Foucault that discourse analysis is essentially comparative, and that we can only understand the significance of what's happening in relation to all other possibilities. Or as Stubbs ([1983]1995) puts it, we can only understand the significance of deviations from the rules when we're aware of them in the first place (p. 57).

In everyday, casual speech, working out what's normal and what counts as a deviation can be difficult. So it's not surprising that researchers have tended to focus on "well-defined and ritualized events" such as greetings, ritual encounters, and even chanting (Coulthard, [1977]1985, p. 59) where it's possible to find an identifiable pattern.

Fortunately for us, educational discourse falls within Coulthard's ([1977]1985) definition of a ritualized event. And as Stubbs ([1983]1995) observes, teaching has traditionally been an obvious choice for discourse analysts since it's not only "highly organized in some rather obvious ways" (p. 40) but also readily available. As a result, numerous studies of educational discourse have been published which not only provide precedents for using particular tools and techniques, but also evidence of patterns of structures and themes typical of education. This gives us a ready-made and reliable basis for comparison.

9: The research

'People are, in general, unused to studying close transcriptions of conversational data. When they do look at such materials, they tend to see them as chaotic or unordered: relative to written texts or to the highly idealized sentences which are data for the grammarian.'[40]

9.1 Data gathering

Over the academic year 2009/10, data for the discourse analysis was collected by observing a tutor group in the Fine Art department of a university. Observation focussed on studio sessions with the tutor since these are unique to Fine Art and the most likely to show interesting discourse deviations.

Both digital recordings and hand-written notes were used to record 19 sessions, from which a sample was selected for the analysis.

One issue that arose was about recording images of the students' artwork, since much of the discourse centred around it. However because of the sensitivity of students about using images of their work in this way, photographs have not been included in the analysis.

9.1.1 Selecting the sample

When it comes to deciding on the right sample size for a particular piece of research, it's a good idea to follow precedents for similar types of work (Clegg, [1982]2003, p. 121). However sample sizes are very variable for discourse analysis, ranging from single events such as a greeting to whole literatures such as Foucault's historical documentation on mental health medical practices.[41] In social science research generally, larger is usually considered to be better, since the larger the sample the more representative it is likely to be (p. 122). Then again the opposite advice may apply to discourse analysis because of the practical dangers of selecting too large a sample and the resulting time it will take for transcription and analysis. Stubbs ([1983]1995) points out that the linguist

---

40 Stubbs, [1983]1995, p. 20

41 Such extremes are not unique to discourse analysis, of course: Clegg ([1982]2003, p. 122) notes that sample size in the social sciences is always controversial, and that although larger is generally assumed to be better, single subject designs can also play an important part for example in psychology.

Noam Chomsky developed many of his theories from analysing fragments in great detail and that "advances in linguistics do not necessarily come from poring over vast amounts of data" (p. 223). For Cameron ([2001]2006, p. 29) it's simple common sense that "while in principle it might seem desirable to have as many examples as possible, in practice you have to draw the line somewhere."

The *principle of adequacy* (Stubbs, [1983]1995, p. 61) refers to the relationship between the sample and the parent population and states that a well-chosen sample will include every part of the variation which exists in the parent population (Clegg, [1982]2003, p. 113), and enough examples of each variation to confirm validity. There are no rules about the minimum set for adequacy, apart from the general guideline that the more that is known about a population, the more accurate the sample is likely to be (p. 115).

Following the principle of adequacy, the sample for this research was chosen to include all formal, tutor-led types of discourse related to studio practice, with more than one example of each type to increase the reliability of the evidence. Timing was also taken into account to ensure that sessions throughout the academic year were included. The discourse analysis sample, with a brief description of each text[42], is given in Table 2.

The sample covers four categories of activity:

- *Category 1: Studio organisation*
  This category consists of sessions where the tutor talks to the students about how to work in the studio and manage their time.

- *Category 2: Student presentations*
  This category consists of sessions where students present their work to both the tutor and their peers and answer questions about it.

- *Category 3: Studio critiques*
  This is probably the most well-known and well-observed form of studio teaching.[43] Three examples of crits are included, two led by the tutor with different year-groups and one involving a visiting tutor.

- *Category 4: One-to-ones*
  This category consists of sessions where the tutor talks privately with students to assess their progress.

---

42 Following Stubbs ([1983]1995), spoken discourse which has been transcribed is referred to as a *text*.

43 For example see Elkins (2001, pp.111-166) who regards the critique as the backbone of contemporary studio education.

9: THE RESEARCH

Category	Date	Title	Description
1 Studio organisation	13/10/09	Text A: The oral brief	The tutor sets the brief for an introductory project for the whole student group
	14/10/09	Text B: The introductory talk	The tutor introduces first year students to the values and practices of working in the studio
	13/1/10	Text C: The studio crisis	The tutor confronts the studio group with their failure to use their studio time appropriately
2 Student presentations	24/11/09	Text D: Student presentations (1)	Students make formal 10-minute presentations to their tutor and peers, followed by discussion
	8/12/09	Text E: Student presentations (2)	As above
3 Studio critiques	17/1/10	Text F Group crit (1)	Year 1 students and the tutor comment on students' work
	24/3/10	Text G Group crit (2)	Year 3 students and the tutor comment on students' work
	24/3/10	Text H: The visiting tutor	A visiting tutor joins the tutor to comment on Year 4 work before their finals
4 One-to-ones	2/5/10	Text I: The one-to-ones	The tutor talks individually to students about their progress

Table 2. The discourse analysis sample.

9.1.2 Preparing the texts for analysis

Our next task was to transcribe the recordings and prepare them as texts for analysis.

In theory it's possible to carry out discourse analysis from audio recordings, but the fugitive and evanescent nature of speech makes this difficult.

> If I say 'hello Rory', by the time I get to *Rory* it is no longer possible to hear hello… recording the utterance does not change this. (Cameron, [2001]2006, p. 31).

For Stubbs ([1983]1995), it's important to represent spoken language as written text for three reasons:

- For accuracy, since our recollections of spoken language are unreliable and subject to the limitations of short-term memory

- For insight, since generally we don't have a clear idea about what spoken language looks like

- For distance, to act as an "estrangement device" and create a necessary distance between the discourse as we experience it and our analysis. This will allow us to see "the complex aspects of conversational coherence which pass us by as real-time conversationalists or observers" (pp. 19-20).

Nevertheless transcription is a far from transparent process, given the differences between spoken language and written text. Spoken language is "evanescent… continuous…and repetitive", full of "false starts, hesitations, repeated words and phrases, and 'fillers' like *well, y'know, like, sort of*" (Cameron, [2001]2006, p. 33), while written language is organised and constructed according to strict rules of grammar. As an example, Stubbs ([1983]1995) compares what people typically say in the aftermath of a traffic accident with the report they submit to their insurance company. Threats, questioning, complaining or swearing are replaced by a neutral, formally organised account (p. 3). This doesn't mean that spoken discourse has no structure of any kind, but that its ordering mechanisms are different and less familiar (p. 19).

So transcription is not just a mechanical task to be carried out by research assistants[44], but an act of interpretation which reflects the instincts or preferences of the researcher. With this in mind, we transcribed the sample texts in line with the recommendations of Stubbs ([1983]1995) and Cameron ([2001]2006), to use the conventions of written text to make the discourse accessible, but to resist the temptation to recast the "elements of chaos" (Stubbs, [1983]1995, p. 20) which are a natural part of spoken discourse into formally correct grammatical structures by completing sentence fragments, removing repetitions, or guessing the sense of words or phrases which appear to be non-sequiturs. Breaks between words were represented conventionally and natural phrasing indicated by a dash, but capital letters, full stops commas or question marks weren't used.

Cameron ([2001]2006, p. 35) reflects on the periodic problem of undecipherable speech, and recommends that any gaps in comprehension are left in the transcript. We followed this advice.

---

44 Stubbs ([1983]1998) quotes Birdwhistell (1970) who calculated that skilled secretaries made one transcription mistake every five words resulting from the attempt to make spoken language fit with the conventions of written text (p. 228).

The transcripts were formatted as numbered lines, with each line allocated to a speaker identified by their role, for example as student, student presenter, tutor, visiting tutor and so on. Different students were identified within each discourse.

9.2 The structural analysis

Decisions about which structural analyses to carry out were made partly on the basis of previous work on educational discourse as a basis for comparison, and partly as a result of the patterns that began to emerge from the data which suggested further investigation. These are described below.

9.2.1 Dominance analysis

Dominance analysis looks at how speech is distributed between the various participants in the discourse. In informal conversation between equals, where authority is shared, we would expect to see a more-or-less equal distribution. In organisational settings, however, we would expect those in roles of authority to dominate.

In fact in classroom settings, where it is a "major part of our commonsense knowledge of classrooms ...that teachers have more power and control than pupils" (Stubbs, [1983]1995, p. 44), research shows that 70 per cent of the lesson is spent in talking, and that 70 per cent of this talk is carried out by the teacher.[45] This pattern reflects the teacher's primary purpose: to "hammer home taken-for-granted fundamentals" (p. 63).

9.2.2 Exchange ratio analysis

According to Coulthard ([1977]1985, p. 64), in informal conversations between equals:

> ...turns to speak are valued and sought and thus the majority of turns in any conversation consist of only a single sentence, unless permission has been sought for a longer turn.

However in more formal settings, where people speak according to preallocated systems, turns tend to be longer as those with authority are allowed to speak for a much longer time.

---

45 Similarly Coulthard ([1977]1985) refers to the "consistent finding" that teachers talk on average for two thirds of talking time (p. 124).

An exchange ratio analysis was carried out for each text to calculate the ratio of turns or exchanges to the length of the text, to give an indication of the average length of exchanges. While we have no precise benchmark figure from existing educational research, we can compare the ratios between texts and infer that the lower the ratio, the more formal the discourse.

9.2.3 Exchange analysis

Exchange structures are about the movement of spoken discourse between people, and provide the fundamental patterns of a given discourse. Coulthard ([1977]1985) follows Sacks in defining conversation as a string of at least two turns, with the first part often predicting what the second part will be: for example questions, greetings, challenges, offers, requests, complaints, invitations and announcements operate in this way. These patterns can allow varying degrees of freedom. For example, a greeting can be followed only by a greeting, but there is more than one kind of response to a complaint. Shorter exchange structures can also be embedded in longer ones, particularly when misapprehension sequences occur, and clarification is needed about the original statement or question before the original exchange structure can regained (p. 69).

Stubbs ([1983]1995) also follows Sacks in taking the basic exchange structure of spoken discourse as a two-part turn defined as an initiation (I) and a response (R) (p. 104). A simple exchange consists of a single turn, while more complex exchanges may be distributed across a number of turns (p. 110). At the start of the exchange sequence possibilities are open-ended but quickly reduce as the shape of the exchange emerges, becoming more elliptic and predictable as it progresses. A new initiation is then introduced which opens up new possibilities. In this sense exchange structures are defined semantically to some extent as they have a relationship to the meaning of the discourse (p. 109).

Informal discourse can make use of any number or variation of exchange patterns with low levels of predictability. However formal discourse is highly predictable, constrained by its distinctive patterns. This is certainly true of educational discourse where "there is quite specific conversational behaviour attached to being a teacher – as teachers would soon discover if they talked to their families as they do to their pupils" (Stubbs [1983]1995, p. 8). Two specific exchange patterns dominate.

The first and most characteristic pattern of traditional educational discourse is what Coulthard ([1977]1985) calls the "powerful three-move structure" of Teacher-Pupil-Teacher (T-P-T) which is so prevalent that the absence of the third part, when it occurs, causes unease and "is often a covert clue that the answer is wrong" (pp. 124-5). Similarly Stubbs ([1983]1995) uses the code Initiation-Response-Feedback (IRF) to describe how the teacher initiates an exchange, elicits a response, and closes down the exchange through feedback, as in the exchange below (p. 131):

T	can you tell me why you eat that food – yes	I
P	to keep you strong	R
T	to keep you strong – yes – to keep you strong	F

The feedback statement is evaluative, which explains the sense of unease noted by Coulthard when it's missing, since students can't be sure about the status of their answers without it.

Variations of the basic structure can occur when parts of the structure are implied rather than articulated. For example the teacher can tell a student to do something, in which case the response is non-verbal, or can ask a question to which the answer does not require evaluative feedback, for example when the teacher asks if students can see the blackboard. The nature of the initiation will determine what follows.

Embedded or misapprehension sequences occur when for example the student has not heard or understood the question, or wants further clarification. Exchanges can also be extended, although rarely: according to Coulthard ([1977]1985), "the exchange is minimally a two-part structure but ...it can consist of up to five moves, though such long exchanges are comparatively rare" (p. 75). These variations don't challenge the underlying patterns of the discourse.

The prevalence of the IRF exchange sequence goes a long way to explaining the dominance analysis finding mentioned above, that teacher talk accounts for 66-70 per cent of classroom discourse, since by definition "the teacher almost always has the last word and two turns to speak for every pupil turn" (Coulthard ([1977]1985, p. 75).

The second characteristic exchange pattern of educational discourse is the one-part exchange or lecture where the teacher imparts information to the students. If students respond at all, it's likely to be by using the meta-communicative feedback response *yes* or *no*. (Stubbs [1983]1995, p. 133). Although a one-part exchange can't technically constitute a discourse, Stubbs argues that the fact that students can potentially respond makes it "intuitively acceptable" to include lectures in educational discourse analysis (p. 139).

Exchange analysis not only shows which patterns are typical of the discourse but also the occasions when they change. Some variations are simply elaborations of the pattern which are accepted as normal by participants, as in the case of miscommunications above.[46] Other variations however may represent a break in the pattern. For example if a student initiates an exchange, fails to respond, or provides feedback to the teacher, a break will have occurred. This might be only a temporary disruption to the discourse, but it's interesting for what it reveals about underlying tensions beneath the surface of the discourse (Stubbs [1983]1995, p. 135).

9.2.4 Interaction analysis

Interaction analysis looks at patterns of turn-taking: who talks to whom and for what proportion of the discourse. This analysis is not usually relevant for educational discourse where the options are limited to teacher-student(s) interactions, with few exceptions. However it soon became clear from the transcripts that interaction patterns were more elaborate than we had anticipated, and worth a closer look.

9.3 The thematic analysis

Thematic analysis is interested in the content of the discourse and in particular what's included and what's excluded. The *principle of completeness* states that all the text in the sample has to be included in this analysis, to avoid the temptation to select only the sections that seem the most relevant or interesting.

Thematic analysis is carried out by an iterative process of coding. Each line of text is ascribed to a theme, and then revisited in the light of the wider pattern of themes which is emerging. It's important to limit codes to a manageable number by grouping themes together wherever possible.

---

46 Although as Stubbs ([1983]1995) observes, miscommunications themselves are always useful to the analyst (p. 57).

10: Structural analysis findings

'It is the task of discourse analysis to study how the script is constructed, and how general taken-for-granted stereotypes of teacher and pupil behaviour are related to the detailed utterance-by-utterance organisation of classroom discourse.'[47]

10.1 Dominance analysis

Results of the dominance analysis are given in Figure 5 below.

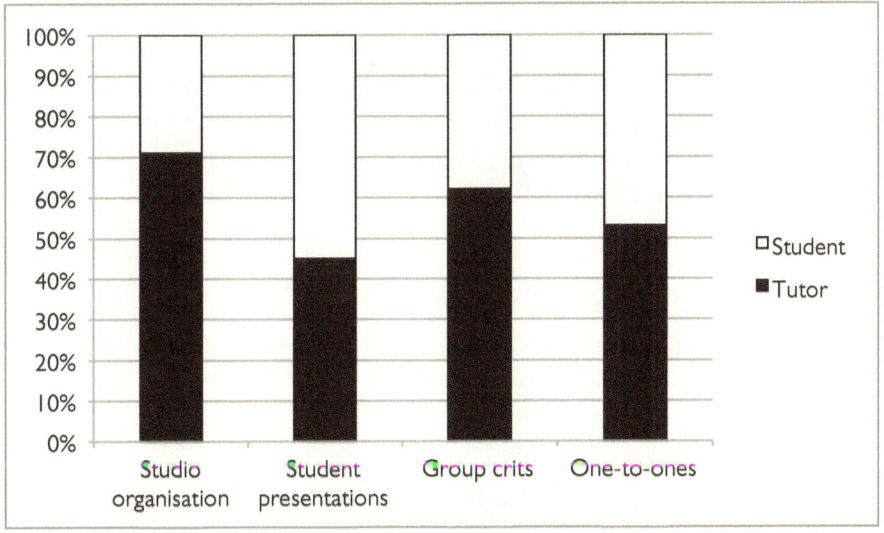

Figure 5. Dominance analysis.

We've said that in traditional educational discourse we would expect to see teacher dominance percentages of around 70%. And indeed this is what we find in the studio organisation texts where the tutor is the authority figure, organising sessions, telling the students what to do and taking the lead in discussions.

But in all the other categories of discourse (student presentations, group crits and one-to-ones), the balance is more equal. Indeed in the student presentations, where students talk about their work and discuss it with an audience

. . . . . .
47 Stubbs, [1983]1995, p. 43

of their peers as well as the tutor, student discourse dominates by 55 per cent to 45 per cent. In these sessions the students have at least as much say as the tutor, even without taking into account the presentations themselves where the student is in the role of lecturer.

In the group crits, where the students display their work to be critiqued by the tutor and their peers, the tutor dominance figure is higher on average at 62%. However this figure is inflated by the presence of a second tutor in one of the crits. When there's only one tutor, she dominates by only a few percentage points. If we take into account the fact that student work forms the subject of the discourse, it's clear that in this core element of Fine Art education, the students have about as much authority as the tutor.

Finally, we can see that in the one-to-one sessions the discourse is distributed evenly between the tutor and the student. As we have seen, this pattern is characteristic of informal conversation, where the speakers allow each other equal roles in the discourse.

So this very first structural analysis tells us that Fine Art teaching is making assumptions that are quite different from those we normally associate with education. In organisational terms, yes, the tutor has authority. But when it comes to knowledge, ideas and opinions, the students have authority too.

10.2 Exchange ratio analysis

Results of the exchange ratio analysis are given in Figure 6 below.

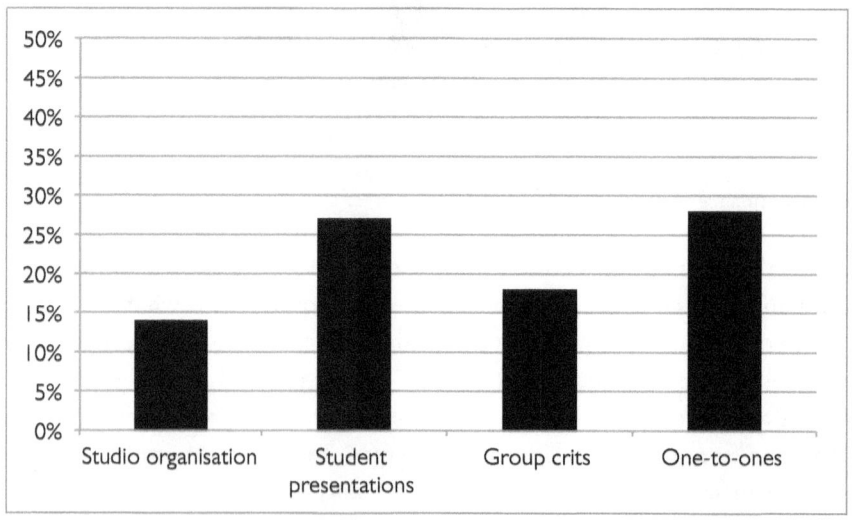

Figure 6. Exchange ratio analysis.

This shows that the average exchange ratio for the studio organisation category is the lowest in the sample. It's comparable to the average of 18% for the studio crit category but much lower than the averages of 27% and 28% for the student presentation category and the one-to-ones respectively. Since lower exchange ratios are associated with the longer exchanges of formal discourse, by this measure, the studio organisation texts are the most formal in the sample. However, they aren't typical. The remaining discourse is, by educational standards, notably discursive and informal.

10.3 Exchange analysis

The exchange analysis chart in Figure 7 below shows the patterns of exchange in the four categories of texts. The codes are explained in the key.

The most striking feature of these results is the range of exchanges in play.

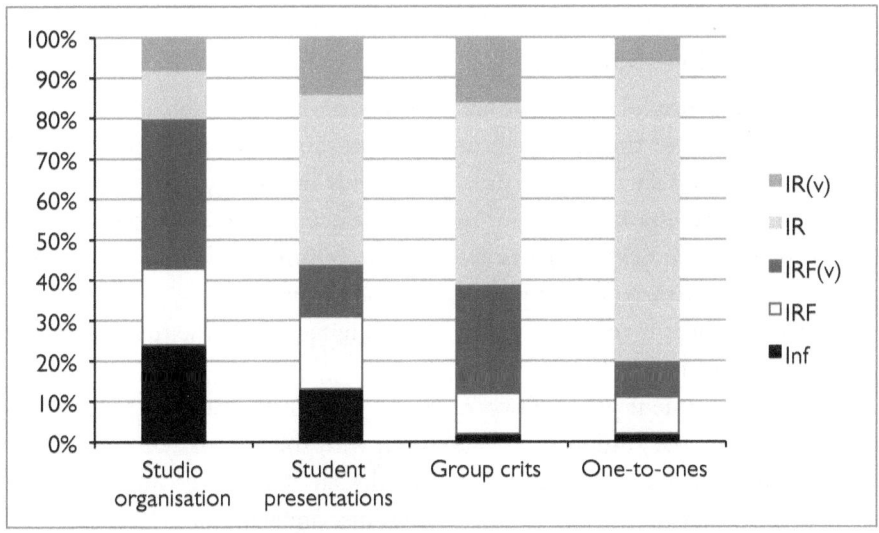

Figure 7. Exchange analysis.

Key

Code	Description
Inf	*Information-giving.* Uninterrupted, one-way discourse as in a lecture.
IRF	*Initiation-Response-Feedback.* The three-part exchange pattern typical of teaching. The teacher normally initiates the exchange and provides feedback.
IRF(v)	*Variations to the Initiation-Response-Feedback pattern.* These might be an extended form of the exchange, feedback might be through a gesture, or there might be multiple responses.
IR	*Initiation-Response* The two-part exchange typical of conversation between equals.
IR(v)	*Variations to the Initiation-Response pattern.* These might be extended exchanges or embedded exchanges within the overall pattern.

10.3.1 Information-giving (Inf)

There are some examples of traditional information-giving or lecturing. For example in the first text, the tutor tells new students about the rules of the studio in an extensive one-way discourse punctuated only by two instances of the meta-communicative response *yes*. Another example occurs in a crit where the tutor responds to a student's experiments with picture-framing with an extemporized discourse on the history of framing and examples from contemporary practice. Overall though there is very little information-giving, where the tutor talks and the students listen passively.

In fact in the student presentation texts, the traditional student-teacher roles are reversed. Here the students have the floor, with the authority to talk about their own work in presentations which they design and deliver themselves. In the discussions that follow, the tutor becomes just one voice among many.

10.3.2 Initiation-Response-Feedback (IRF)

The distinctive Initiation-Response-Feedback (IRF) pattern is also well represented. For example in the sequence below, the tutor initiates a question which is answered by one of the students and to which she then provides corrective feedback, in classic teaching style.

10: STRUCTURAL ANALYSIS FINDINGS

T	...what I want is a title sequence – do you know where [these phrases] came from	I
S1	lyrics from songs	R
T	song titles actually	F

However this is by no means the dominant style in any of the texts. And as in the information-giving analysis above, there are also examples of the students taking the initiation and occasionally even the feedback role. The example below shows how both the students and the tutor evaluate a particular artwork (and fortunately for the students, agree).

S2	it's something mesmerizing	R
S3	it's an improvement from before – better when it's faster – I think a little bit more – and maybe shorter	F
T	it's a vast improvement…it's fabulous	F

It's hard to imagine the average lecturer's reaction if a student started not only asking the questions but evaluating the answers as well, as in the extract below.

S1	what artists have you looked at in terms of memories	I
S2	none	R
S1	there's an exhibition at the Barbican you should see	F

10.3.3 Variations to Initiation-Response-Feedback (IRF(v))

Variations to the IRF pattern arise when the exchange is extended, perhaps to explore a point further as in the example below (the code *Ic* is used to indicate a continuation of the initiation).

S1	why have you diversified like this	I
S2	I don't know it's better than before I think	R
S1	why	Ic
S2	these are deep questions	F

The tutor uses this pattern when she wants students to explore questions themselves rather than relying on her for the answers which she clearly knows.

T	…what do you think?	I
S	anything in London is so expensive	R
T	why	Ic
S	the people who come are buyers	R
T	how much do you have to make	Ic
S	more	R
T	it is an alien concept – but it's all part of the same concept	F

One interesting variation is the response-to-feedback move, where the tutor seems to close down the exchange with a feedback statement only to find the student responding to the feedback as an initiation and necessitating a further feedback move.

T	it's easy to look at an image – it's an abject setting – not considered – it's a non-space – cutting out the phone is terminal – it has to be in real time – it's the integrity of the piece	F
P	the first 15 minutes was real time – then we guessed the length of time – we didn't know how to get it across	R
T	the intention is not the same as the effect – the staring thing – the compromise – the visual thing is what the viewer sees	F

Here the first feedback statement is a forceful judgement on the artwork ("cutting out the phone is terminal…it's the integrity of the piece") and structurally terminal. However the student choses to read it instead as an initiation and responds by explaining why the problem happened ("we didn't know how to get it across") so that the tutor has to find a second feedback move ("the intention is not the same as the effect") in order to finally close the exchange.

These variations are indicative of a sophisticated discourse which goes way beyond the simple imparting of information. Instead, the tutor and her students are questioning and exploring ideas to which there are no obvious or easy answers.

10: STRUCTURAL ANALYSIS FINDINGS

10.3.4 Initiation-Response (IR)

With the exception of the studio organisation texts, the dominant pattern of discourse is the conversational initiation-response (IR). Sometimes these exchanges are for simple fact-finding, as in the example below.

S	actual work or photos	I
T	actual work unless it is the photos	R

More typically, however, they represent the rapid conversational flow that often results from students talking to each other. Given that students seem wary of using the teacherly feedback move, it's perhaps not surprising that they prefer this form of exchange. In the example below, the sequence of exchanges only ends when the tutor intervenes with a remark which acts structurally as a feedback move (F), although it isn't particularly evaluative.

S6	what about another part of the body – maybe a casting of limbs	I
S2	it's hard to do a performance with limbs	R
S5	do you start with a face and create a character – are narrative skills important	I
S2	yes – it's like assessing a fiction	R
S4	have you thought of works more specific to performance	I
S2	I want to – characters or animals or with subtle distinctions	R
S1	could you perhaps put implants in people's face	I
S2	I want to – characters or animals or with subtle distinctions	R
T	or a head or an ear or an arm	F

The tutor can be involved in these exchanges either as initiator or respondent, structurally indistinguishable from her students as in the example below.

T	is there a difference between the shoes and the red peppers	I
S2	yes – manmade and natural forms – like still life paintings where there's a single idea – I wanted to try something different	R
S	did you work from peppers or photos	I
S2	some are from images – some are for real	R

10.3.5 Variations to Initiation-Response (IR(v))

The final kind of exchange represents variations to the Initiation-Response pattern (IR(v)). As with variations to the IRF pattern, these occur from more complex exchanges, perhaps with multiple initiators or responders, or extended discussions of difficult ideas. The example below shows how complex such variations can be.

S1	I think the small shapes correlate with each other – successful – but then it's hard – it might be better higher up – not so successful	R
S2	the correlation – it's like a fractal or something – like nature – the repetition of patterns – I'm not sure if it's intentional	R
T	about the presentation – is the floor the best place – we want to see the best contrast	R
S3	the colour works well	R
T	power – the rock	R
S3	not sure about the little ones – they take away from the large one – if it was really big it would be great – really impressive	R
S4	the form's seductive – clever – it's sort of flowing – the little ones take away from it though – you could make it large so you could walk through the middle – the form and the colour is seductive and powerful	R
S5	the colour's intriguing – the form has integrity – there could be more little ones though – what about a marriage between the post-its and the larger paper	

Here the artwork the students are looking at can be seen structurally as initiating the discourse. In the sequence that follows, the students and the tutor are partly responding to each other (S1: I think the small shapes correlate with each other…; S2: the correlation – it's like a fractal or something) but also to the implicit initiating question posed by the artwork. The three strands of the exchange about the shapes, colour, and presentation of the sculpture interweave with each other. In this exchange more ideas are introduced than are resolved, and the role of the tutor as respondent shows again how authority is distributed across role boundaries. Sophisticated indeed!

10: STRUCTURAL ANALYSIS FINDINGS

	Code	Theme	Description
1	TR	Tutor's role and responsibilities	The tutor's explanation of her role and text which implies it in statements such as "stop talking you two"
2	SR	Students' role and responsibilities	Both direct discussion between the students and the tutor and text which implies the students' role such as the meta-communicative response "OK"
3	SC	Studio culture	Direct discourse about how the studio should and does work
4	SD	Studio discourse	Direct discussion about the language the students do or should use in the studio
5	O	Operational concerns	How the studio space is managed and how and when the students and the tutor will work there
6	TT	Tools and techniques	Discussions about how to handle both materials (for example paint or latex) and technologies (for example photography or film)
7	B	Project brief	A set project where the tutor gives the students the task of making a film from a song title as a warm-up exercise
8	P	Professional practice	Issues to do with the students as practising artists in the commercial world
9	R	Research	The sources which students use to inform their work, including both other artists and other disciplines
10	I	Intentions	Discourse relating to the students' artworks with a focus on meaning: the ideas which inform it and which it communicates
11	F	Form	Discourse relating to the students' artworks with a focus on shape, colour, composition, and presentation
12	D	Documentation	Discourse relating to the written work students prepare to accompany their artwork as part of the examination process.

Table 3. Themes and their descriptions.

10.4 Interaction analysis

The final analysis looks at who talks to whom. The results of the interaction analysis are shown in Figure 8 below. The codes are explained in the key.

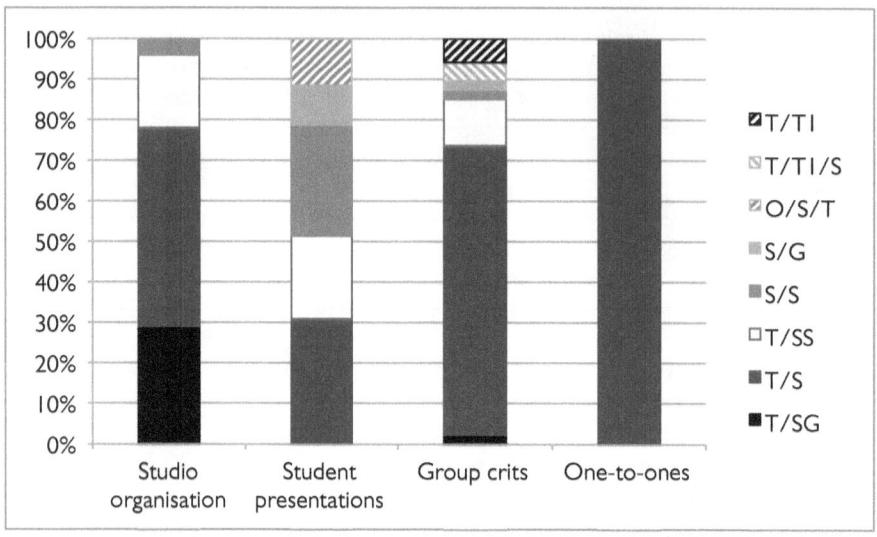

Figure 8. Interaction analysis.

Key

Code	Description
T/SG	Discourse between the tutor and the student group as a whole.
T/S	Discourse between the tutor and one particular student.
T/SS	Discourse between the tutor and a series of students.
S/S	Discourse between students.
S/G	Discourse between a student and the student group as a whole.
O/S/T	Discourse between the art object, students and the tutor.
T/TI/S	Discourse between the tutor, a visiting tutor and the students.
T/TI	Discourse between the tutor and the visiting tutor.

In a traditional teaching situation, we would expect the discourse to be limited to exchanges between the teacher and the class as a whole, or between the teacher and a student picked by the teacher.

There is something of this pattern in the studio organisation texts, where most of the exchanges are between the tutor and either the group as a whole, a particular student, or a series of students. Even in these relatively conventional texts, however, we can see something unusual – legitimated discourse between students (S/S) which acknowledges that students have something worthwhile to say to each other.

In the student presentations texts, more possibilities emerge. Here, in addition to the exchange patterns above, we can see students addressing their peers as a group (S/G), and conversations involving the students' art objects which, structurally, initiate the discourse (O/S/T).

In the group crits, most of the discourse is between the tutor and individual students. In one text, the presence of a visiting tutor adds to an already complex set of possibilities. Now not only do the tutors talk to the students but also each other, to elaborate on each others' points and also, on occasion, to disagree.

By definition, of course, discourse in the one-to-ones is between the tutor and individual students.

As in the exchange analysis above, the interaction analysis shows a highly complex set of discourse possibilities, with which the tutor seems very comfortable to the extent of consistently encouraging them. Indeed in the extract below she celebrates her student's assertiveness:

S	I really like it – I think it's really good – when you say you are confused with the direction I completely disagree – I can see straight away
T	oh I'm so proud

10.5 Structural analysis and the Framework of Educational Assumptions

It's clear that the discourse of studio teaching shows few of the structural characteristics of traditional classroom teaching. There's no single point of authority, no one answer to the questions under consideration. This gives rise to a complex set of discourse possibilities where everyone's view may be legitimate, whether or not the tutor agrees.

Mapping the results of the structural analysis to the Framework of Educational Assumptions makes the connection between the structure of the discourse and the kind of teaching it allows. Figure 9 below shows a rich picture representation of what these connections might be.

136 ART AS EXTRAORDINARY SCIENCE

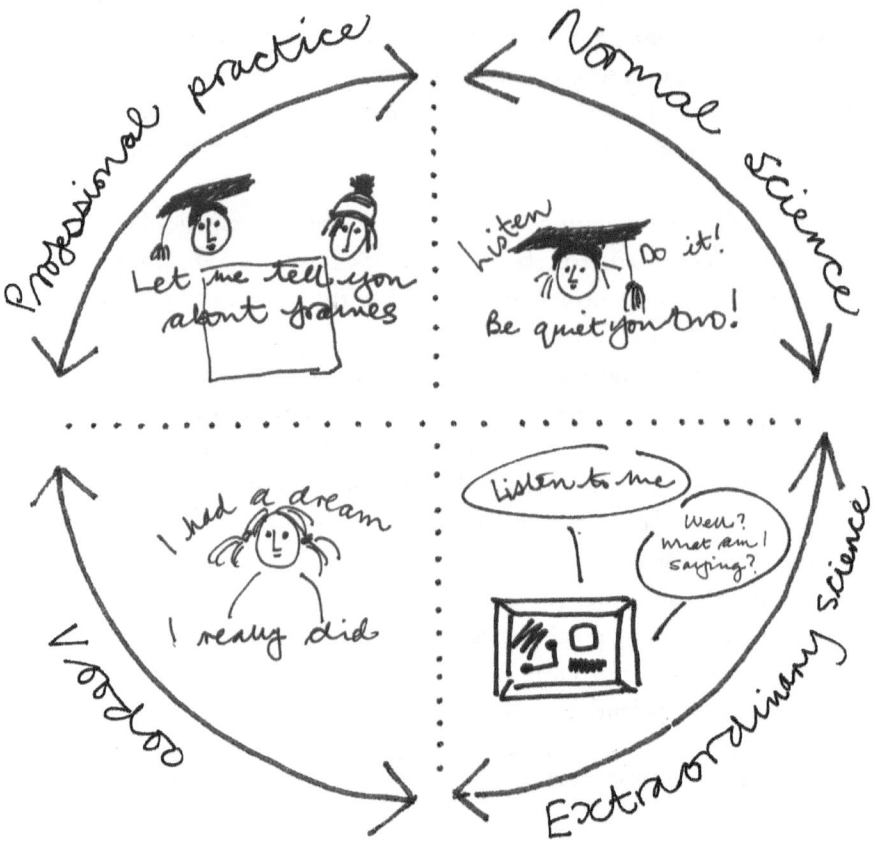

Figure 9. A rich picture representation of the relationship between the structural analysis and the Framework of Educational Assumptions.

10.5.1 Normal Science

The Normal Science quadrant is represented by the image of the tutor in an academic hat as a symbol of authority who controls the discourse. Traditional educational discourse structures such as lecturing and information-response-feedback exchange patterns belong to this quadrant where teaching is characterised by passing on the "constellation of beliefs, values, techniques and so on" for the particular discipline (Kuhn, [1962]1970, p. 175) and where the role of the student is to listen and agree.

We can see that these structures are used from time to time, notably when the studio organisation texts begin with the tutor's authoritative "stop talking

10: STRUCTURAL ANALYSIS FINDINGS

you two". There's also evidence of the traditional structures when for example the tutor sets the rules of the crits, evaluates the students' work, emphasises learning points, challenges attitudes or performance, makes references to exam requirements, and so on.

10.5.2 Professional Practice

The Professional Practice quadrant is represented by an image of the tutor looking at the student's work and contributing complementary information, in this case about the history of framing.

Structurally, this occurs when the information-giving structure associated with lectures and seminars is integrated into the ongoing discourse, to making the connection between theory and practice and apply historical or technical information to specific practical problems.

10.5.3 Extraordinary Science

The Extraordinary Science quadrant is represented by the image of a student's artwork on display, commanding our attention and posing the implicit question "what am I saying?"

Here the discourse is initiated and sustained by ideas which are articulated and presented but not, or not yet, formally known or accepted. The task of exploring and analysing the artworks is shared between the students and the teacher with equal authority because the work is new, and there can be no pre-existing knowledge to give the tutor the advantage.

10.5.4 Voodoo

The Voodoo quadrant is represented by the image of a student talking about her dreams. This kind of wholly subjective discourse is allowed by the structure of the student presentations, where students are free to explore the inspiration behind their work.

S	with the mythology your work is based on – I'm interested in how you relate to myth – how real it was to you – half of you says history and mythology – half of you that this is something that should still be around
S1	because a lot of it is history – it is a belief in a way – a belief system not a religion with rules – I did have a deeper belief doing the research – we look outward – transcendence – so its more of a relocation – looking back into the human body – its something I believed in – to look more internally – so its played a big role in what I'm doing

11: Thematic analysis findings

'…it is a general rule about conversation that it is your business not to tell people what you can suppose they know…conversationalists…constantly analyse what is said for its newsworthiness, 'why that now and to me'…'[48]

11.1 Identifying the themes

Identifying themes from the texts was an iterative process which involved coding each line of text to make sure there was no bias in the analysis. A certain amount of subjectivity was involved in allocating the codes, for example in distinguishing between *Operational concerns* and the *Tutor's role and responsibilities*, since part of the tutor's role involves operational matters, or between *Studio culture* and *Students' role and responsibilities*, since the students are responsible for the studio culture. To minimise the impact of this subjectivity, the texts were coded twice. The comparatively large size of the sample also helped to ensure that the impact of any one coding decision was minimised.

The 12 themes that resulted from the analysis is shown in Table 3 below. The first five themes (*Tutor's role and responsibilities, Students' role and responsibilities, Studio culture, Studio discourse,* and *Operational concerns*) are about how the work of the studio is managed and organised. The final six (*Project brief, Professional Practice, Research, Intentions, Form, Documentation*) relate to the students' work. *Tools and techniques* relates to both.

11.2 Theme descriptions

The following descriptions summarise the discourse around each theme.

11.2.1 Tutor's role and responsibilities (TR)

From her opening words in Text A, "stop talking you two" it's clear that the tutor has a traditional role as an authority figure who's responsible for the studio and its arrangements. Throughout the texts the tutor is busy with tasks such as organising sessions of various kinds, arranging for presentations to be recorded or drumming up support for the student presentations.

---
48 Coulthard ([1977]1985, p. 79

However the tutor is simultaneously keen to distance herself from this traditional role, as she explains to the new students. Rather than just telling the students what to do, she's there to encourage them to take responsibility for their own development. This is the role of the coach[49], who is committed to doing whatever it takes to "get as much out of you and your practice as possible".

T   …don't see it as me giving and you taking – that's your parents' job – I'm the catalyst to give cohesion…

In this role, the tutor's responsibility is to encourage her students to be productive. As a practising artist herself, she focuses the students on making artworks and keeping up with current practice through visiting exhibitions and galleries.

A further and more difficult role is of the tutor as critic. This aspect of Fine Art teaching has had a somewhat notorious history and for Elkins (2001) the problem persists in contemporary critiques which, subject as they are to the whims and eccentricities of the tutor, may often seem like "veiled psychodramas" (p. 134). The tutor acknowledges to her new students that "some of you will find the criticism difficult so I apologise now" while at the same time emphasising that "it's not personal…I don't want to upset you…I want to get as much out of you as possible". Throughout the texts general comments such as "you could work a little bit harder", "you need to engage", or "you need to come up to the mark" are commonplace, at times reducing the students to silence, as in the example below.

T   …I'm not going anywhere with it – an elegant little side table with a value for money mat underneath and I am stuck at that… *(silence)*…a little harsh I appreciate but this is where I have to be responsible…I have to take responsibility

---

The role of the tutor as critic also involves developing the students' ability to critique each other. For example, when the students fail to comment on the obviously racial overtones of a particular artwork, the tutor takes them to task for their inability to confront difficult issues.

Uncomfortable as it may be on occasion, the students accept the role of the tutor as critic and see its value. One student is philosophical in her response:

---

49 The role of the coach is familiar from the world of sport, where "sports coaches assist athletes in developing to their full potential. They are responsible for training athletes in a sport by analysing their performances, instructing in relevant skills and by providing encouragement…the role of the coach is to create the right conditions for learning to happen and to find ways of motivating the athletes. Therefore, you can see that it is a very difficult task and requires a very special person." (Retrieved December 12, 2013, from www.topendsports.com)

"I definitely wouldn't do it this way again – I'm not going to defend it" while another is glad to have her own reservations about her work confirmed: "I'm too close – I can understand they're not successful – I need them to go up and get criticism – I disliked them".

And of course critique can also be praise: the tutor also knows how to give credit.

Interestingly however the tutor threatens to withdraw from both the roles of traditional teacher and coach in Text C, *The studio crisis*, when she accuses the students of failing to establish the right kind of studio culture. If the instincts of a traditional teacher would be to put in more time with students who are underperforming, the tutor's response is the opposite. Instead of adopting a parental role which will turn the students into children, she cancels seminars and crits for the following two weeks to give the students time and space to think about what they want. This text provides insight into some of the paradoxes of the tutor's role whereby more investment by the tutor results in less by the students, and where the way to fix the role is to make it disappear.[50] An important part of the tutor's role would seem to be about managing the tensions between support and dependency.

11.2.2 Students' role and responsibilities (SR)

Much of the discourse around the students' responsibilities reflects traditional educational values, and in particular hard work. According to the tutor, "the most important thing is to stick to your practice". This involves effort ("…it's a lot of work – lot lot lot lot"), productivity ("stuff is what I want – hard stuff is a vital tool"), and visible progress ("I want to see progress – changing every time"). Students who work hard win approval while those who don't are courting failure: "for one who didn't come in – she had nothing done – there's no point in continuing". In fact the studio crisis in Text C is triggered by what the tutor sees as the students' lack of productivity: "there's not enough work being done – fact – none of you produce enough or work hard enough".

Related to hard work are the university's degree requirements, for example by preparing presentations and documentation, and taking part in the final show, all of which are to be taken seriously.

Yet if the general principle of productivity is non-negotiable, the work the students do, when, where, and how much is up to them. Intellectually too the

------

50 The power of the tutor's deliberate absence is something known by the Bauhaus and Michael Asher at CalArts, for example, where the space left by the tutor's authority becomes the creative vacuum to be filled by the students.

students have authority, as the tutor admits: "mine's only one opinion – a lot of you have more interesting experiences – they're all valid – they're as important as my opinion".

In the exchange below we can see how new students struggle to understand what this autonomy means, used as they are to set projects and what the tutor refers to as "heavily tutored prescribed courses".

S3	I want something to work with
S4	if you let us do what we want what do we do – go – or do we do whatever we want
S2	do we jump in and you give us guidance
S5	are there no set projects

In her reflections on art as research, artist Siún Hanrahan describes the pressure of this unique responsibility.

> An empty studio is a demand: 'Come, let us mean some meaning, let us think some thoughts.' To respond and get to work is to overcome the obstacle of 'which thoughts and why?' And to do this in the face of the fact that neither the studio nor anything else can ground the answer; there is no justification outside of your own choice. There is a space to be filled with thinking and you must make a start, somewhere, and keep going, in some direction…it is all a matter of choice. You are the warrant of your work, of the meanings you make…you must simply keep going through making choices…or not." (Hanrahan, 2006, p. 144)

Finally, the students have a role as critics both of their own and each other's work. This role is partly altruistic, insofar as the students give up their time to support their peers. The role of critic also relates to the students' own work, as it is through this role that they learn how their work will be judged and how to defend it. As the tutor explains:

T	you will get as much out of listening to somebody else speaking about their work … as you do about yourself…remember we're building tools that we need to make us more successful makers or doers or thinkers – so you listen to what other people are saying…

As we saw in the structural analysis, the students as critics are happy to initiate and discuss but are less confident about giving feedback. Student authority has its limits.

Text C: *The studio crisis* is an example of the tensions that can arise due to the different roles and responsibilities of the students. While the tutor wants the students to work in the studio more, the students are clear about their responsibility to work in the way that suits them best. Some agree with the tutor's arguments and promise to come in more, but others remain unpersuaded, either because it's easier to work at home with their own equipment, because it's quieter and less distracting, or because working in different environments provides inspiration.

In a paradox of studentship, students are expected to be at once conformist and autonomous, obedient and independent.

11.2.3 Studio culture (SC)

In Text A the tutor introduces the new students to her ideal of what the studio culture should be: a highly socialized environment where students are inspired by the common cause of their art practice. The introductory project is the new students' opportunity to learn this culture, buddying with older students, sharing technical expertise, and learning to work together in a supportive social atmosphere: "I would like to think that if I asked for a cup of coffee you would do that for me".

However we've seen from the analysis of the students' role above that students make their own decisions about how they work, often quite rationally. So we need to ask why the tutor is so upset by the students who choose to work away from the studio.

The answer may lie in the tutor's commitment to the paradigm of her own studio experience: "I mean when I went to college I went in everyday and so was everyone else – it was a great environment – a great social time – just a given". The fact that the students are now choosing to work differently represents a paradigm shift which will inevitably be characterised by a sense of crisis with a polarization between "competing camps or parties, one seeking to defend the old institutional constellation, the other seeking to institute some new one" (Kuhn, [1962]1970, pp. 297).

11.2.4 Studio discourse (SD)

Studio discourse refers to the language of the studio and the way in which the students are taught to talk about their work.

For the tutor, studio discourse represents "the voice of the artist" which is otherwise absent from the lectures and seminars of the Fine Art degree. This isn't a considered or formal kind of discourse, but a spontaneous and wide-ranging way of talking which includes "silly or stupid – intellectual spiritual disparate things", and represents an "intimate dialogue" between the artists and their work. This characterisation of studio discourse is supported by the structural analysis above, where conversational forms predominate.

Art like any other discipline has its own jargon, in this case derived from the languages of philosophy and psychoanalysis, but for the tutor this kind of formal artspeak is inappropriate for talking about the students' artworks. The occasions where students use this kind of conceptual language are not rewarded, as in the exchange below:

T	what do you mean
S1	as R uses a photograph – referential familiarity – it has a connotation to it – wishing for it to be how it's characterised – the motif is a source generalisation
T	these are huge grand statements – where is the motif

Here the tutor not only rejects the critical language used by the student in favour of her own ordinary language questions "what do you mean…where is the motif", but is also dismissive of the student's "huge grand statements" which tell her nothing about the work itself.

Similarly, in her introduction to the visiting tutor from whom she expects a more formal critical discourse, the tutor distances herself from it:

T	if there are words that T1 uses that you don't understand please all of you have enough confidence to say I don't understand – cause I can hold my hand up and say I don't understand either…don't feel intimidated and don't feel that you can't say I don't understand that word…so please do not be intimidated

It seems clear that the tutor doesn't see the language of art criticism as appropriate for studio discourse, or intend the students to learn it there. Her preference for pragmatic rather than critical terms fits with McGilchrist's (2009) analysis of the sources of different kinds of language. According to McGilchrist, language is the province of both the left and right hemispheres of the brain, with the left responsible for syntax and vocabulary, the "nitty-gritty" of language, and the right for its expressive, interpretive qualities. The language of the right brain is "embodied and largely intuitive" (p. 121), an expression of spontaneous emotions and intuitions which McGilchrist associates with the skills of music and dance:

> …a bodily skill, further, that is acquired by each of us through imitation, by the emotional identification and intuitive harmonisation of the bodily states of the one

who learns with the one from whom it is learnt; a skill moreover that originates in the brain as an analogue of bodily movements, and involves the same processes, and even the same brain areas, as certain highly expressive gestures...that anthropologists see as derived from music. (McGilchrist, 2009, p. 122)

From this perspective the tutor's association of spontaneous language with the making of the artwork is right. Language from the left brain, the "organ of reason" (McGilchrist, 2009, p. 113), comes later, after the work is done.

The recurring theme of the use of the word *like* provides insight into the limits of spontaneity, however. Students are prohibited from using the term and may be corrected when they do, as in the extract below.

S2	I-I was just about to say I like it – but
T	don't

As an alternative, students are taught to say that work is "successful" or "unsuccessful", since personal taste is not the issue.

T	I need you to learn a language that enables you to articulate yourself in a way that's well foundationed – well grounded – and is not about like and dislike because that's – you know I like LA – kind of – does it mean anything – who cares

Spontaneous as it may be, studio discourse is wary of the purely subjective.

11.2.5 Operational concerns (O)

Operational concerns relate to how the studio is organised. Students are called to attend and to attention, split into groups, given timetables and deadlines, and pointed in the direction of necessary resources; rooms are booked, IT equipment made available and timetable issues resolved.

At times however the students are expected to take operational responsibility themselves. One example is choosing studio space based on nicely ambiguous advice. On the one hand, students need to be sensible and pay attention to the rules and regulations. On the other hand, they should also show initiative and reject conventional ideas of what a studio space looks like: "don't have too many tables and chairs – it's a kind of security", including taking the outside space into account: "notice the external doors – it's a glorious day – work outside".

The question of who makes operational decisions is not always clear to the students, and they can get into trouble for example with technical support staff.

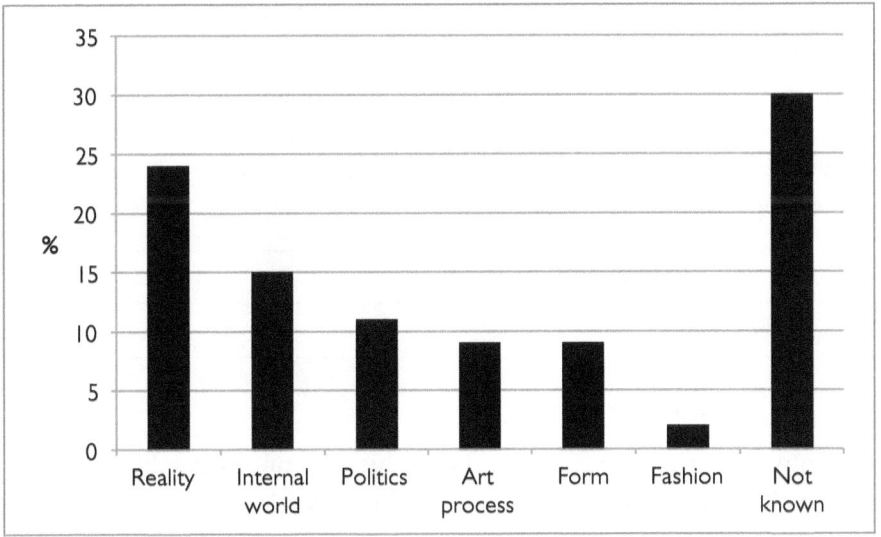

Figure 10. A classification of student artworks by intention.

The studios may seem like free-and-easy spaces without rules, but it is simply that the rules are often ambiguous and hard to see.

11.2.6 Tools and techniques (TT)

The theme of tools and techniques refers to the development of the practical and technical skills students need to create their artworks.

This raises the issue of technology and its role in creating artworks. The tutor is keen for students to use modern technologies confidently in their practice and expects students to be proactive about learning from studio technicians or each other, a point explicitly made by the induction project of making a video. Technology is an extension of capability: "I don't want it limited by your abilities."

Although the tutor doesn't make a connection between new technologies and changes in studio culture, it's worth reflecting on Bruno Latour's point that "the questions to ask about any agent are simply the following: Does it make a difference in the course of some other agent's action or not?" (Latour, [2005]2007, p. 71). To judge if technology makes a difference, we can compare the student painter who is most likely to work in the studio because their work isn't portable and studio space elsewhere is hard to find with the student film-maker who may be out of the studio on a number of counts: arranging actors, finding and using locations, processing and screening. The need for students to be confident users of technology is at odds with the tutor's model of studio-based practice and a likely contributor to the paradigm shift. Indeed of the 46 artworks in the research texts, 10 (22%) were film.

In general, students are responsible for developing their own repertoire of tools and techniques and the tutor isn't sympathetic to failures of technique, as in the example below.

T	it bugs me – the furrowing is not cut off…
SP13	it's badly made

11.2.7 The project brief (B)

There's only one example of a project brief which the tutor gives the students as part of their induction and which involves filming a title sequence around song titles she provides.

In presenting the brief, the tutor is concerned with challenging the students to be original. She chooses song titles that are deliberately obscure and "something outside your eye and cultural engagement…something you can't stylise or project". The project also represents a social opportunity for the students to get to know each other, and an opportunity to get up to speed with video technology.

Overall however the importance of the project is deliberately downplayed. The brief itself is delivered orally with few instructions. The tutor refers to the project as "a small exercise – no complications" which is not to be taken too seriously. This tone is reflected back by one of the students in her comment, "it's a nice little exercise".

The reason for downplaying the brief in this way is because of the distinction between work which results from a problem set by some one else and work which is generated by the students themselves. Artworks have to originate with the students themselves. In the exchange below, we can see how new students struggle to understand what this means.

S3	I want something to work with
S4	if you let us do what we want what do we do – go – or do we do whatever we want
S2	do we jump in and you give us guidance
S5	are there no set projects

11.2.8 Professional practice (P)

The theme of professional practice is introduced when the tutor talks to the students about their future as artists and the importance of the professional art market. Although many of the students have no aspirations to be professional artists and are considering alternatives such as teaching or art therapy[51], the tutor teaches them as though they are.

This is the tradition of professions to "teach to the top", noted by Philips in her study of the language socialization of lawyers, where students are taught courtroom language although most will never use it: "thus we see in legal instruction not the most common activities, but rather the most influential activities of the profession" (1982, p. 194). For the tutor, for as long the students are students, they are also artists.[52]

11.2.9 Research (R)

The theme of research refers to the sources of information from which the students draw in creating and documenting their work.

For the students, research is an accepted part of the process of developing their work and is recorded in the documentation which accompanies their artwork for assessment.

In theory any objects or ideas can be cited as research. As the tutor says:

> T …a reference point shouldn't always be corralled by art either historical or contemporary or otherwise – remember we need to make reference to fashion – design – you know everywhere – cinema – those are really important

In practice, research in the texts mostly refers to one of three categories: other disciplines, art galleries, and other artists.

Other disciplines

Since students are free to work in any area that interests them, it follows that their research may take them to any other discipline which seems relevant. For one student, this means is psychology and the theory of memory; for another, the disciplines are history and mythology.

---

51 From the tutor group of 10 students, four are interested in the art market, three are "kind of" interested, and three are not.

52 This compares with tutor Dennis Adams' practice of treating students "more as young practitioners than as students going through a programme. There's this sense that first and foremost we're a community of working artists" (Adams, Bos, & Haacke, 2009, p. 260).

In their paper *Artereality* which aims to "contribute to repositioning arts education closer to the centre of the contemporary knowledge economy" (p. 143), Stanford professors Schnapp and Shanks (2009) see the "transdisciplinary reach" of art research as remarkable in the context of standard academic practice, where the boundaries of specialist knowledge are so firmly maintained. Certainly in the examples above, the students are able to move confidently across disciplinary boundaries for the purposes of their practice.

Art galleries

The emphasis throughout the texts on the importance of visiting art galleries and exhibitions is partly to make students aware of the contemporary art market, but partly also to provide contemporary connections with their own work.

Other artists

The most frequent discourse relating to research concerns other artists, characterised by a constant exchange of references between the tutor and students and between students.

Research may be necessary, but it's not enough to make a successful artwork. Finding the right relationship between the work of other artists and the students' individual practice can be complex. For the students it's important not to be naïve in referencing other artists. As the tutor remarks:

> T   where you show images of A in your documentation you're not just showing images of A – you're actually tapping into an ongoing discussion and critical debate about these artists that you are going to be exposed to whether you like it or not

At a practical level, other artists can provide students with ideas about how to approach particular problems. This can also mean learning from other artists' mistakes. In the example below, the tutor relates a student's problems with designing access to their interactive installation to similar problems with an installation at the Tate, so that the student can learn from both failures.

> T   …do you not think all these large institutions that we feel are the pinnacle of what have you – they don't always get it right either

However if students follow the work of others too closely, they risk becoming derivative. In one example, when the tutor makes a direct connection between the student's approach and that of the artist P, the student's work is invalidated: "P did it for a documentary – it's not new".

Choosing to reinterpret past work can also be a problem. In the example below, the student's citing of artist A as a source leads to comparisons which undermine her own work. While the student is interested in the form of A's work, the tutor sees the "troublingness" of A's subjects as integral, making the student's work seem superficial by comparison.

> T1   you've mentioned A in your work but a lot of her work is really troubling – the characters she's photographing are posing questions about the society in which we live and if you were then to give your lightness of touch to these kinds of photographs there would be more of a tension…

An example of the limitations of research in making successful art occurs when a student's installation is under review. When the tutor asks the student to explain it, her response is in many ways exemplary, an informed explanation of her research.

> P2   …it's because I was reading BR's the conquest of happiness and the titles on the words of the thing are the titles from the chapters envy being the most prominent one because it drew together all my work – it brought together the idea of the mother's role and later on in life the wife's role and brings the feminist element into it – it was basically saying it was necessary for happiness

In spite of this explanation however the tutor sees the installation as failing, leading to the warning that "sometimes people use words – they think somehow it's there but that doesn't make it art".

11.2.10 Intentions (I)

Discourse about intentions focuses on the ideas behind the artworks, the result of Hanrahan's (2006) solitary struggle with "which thoughts and why".

Intentions may be more or less complex and require different degrees of teasing out, but ultimately we need to be able to find them. The tutor's main reason for disliking the artwork in the extract below is that she can't see the ideas behind it:

> T   I'm not convinced by the presentation – it's thin…it needs another dimension – it doesn't ask any questions – it is what it is – it doesn't transcend anything… I'm not going anywhere with it – it doesn't allow me to ask questions

While every student's intentions are different, it's possible to see themes emerging across the 46 student artworks discussed in the texts. Figure 10 below shows a classification of the artworks by intention.

This analysis shows that:

- The largest category *Reality* (24%) includes artworks whose intention is to play with our understanding of reality and show us something different about the world we think we know
- The second largest category of intentions can be described as *Internal World* (15%) where students explore our internal landscapes such as dreams, memory or the psychology of waiting
- Five of the artworks (11%) have political intentions with feminism the most common
- Four artworks (9%) are interested in the process of making the artwork rather than the work itself
- Four artworks (9%) have the exploration of form as their intention
- For fourteen of the artworks, intentions are either not discussed or identified as absent. Absence of intention is always a problem.

From this sample we can see the difficulties students often have with either finding or articulating their intentions, particularly when complex political issues are involved, and the importance of the crit for testing their validity and how well they communicate.

11.2.11 Form (F)

Discourse around form focuses on the physical dimensions of the artworks. Figure 11 below shows three themes emerging from the analysis: description, analysis, and variation.

11: THEMATIC ANALYSIS FINDINGS

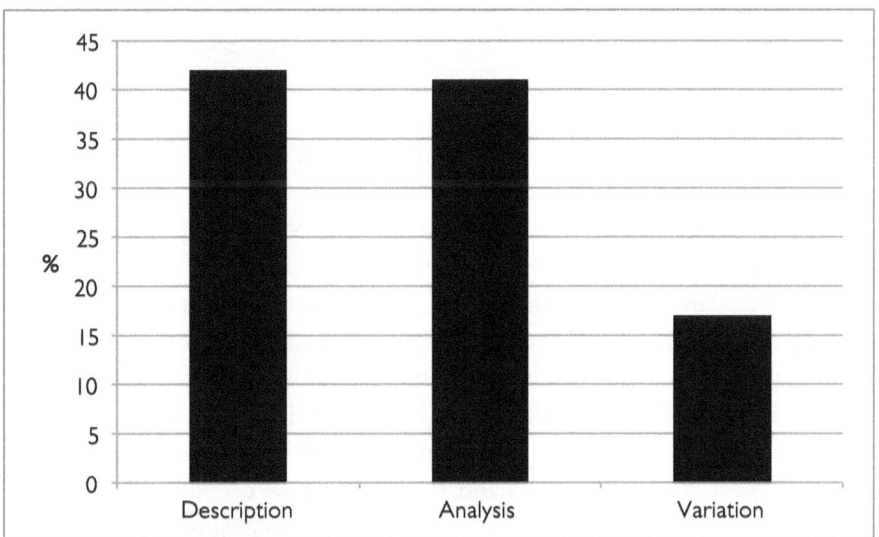

Figure 11. Themes emerging from the discourse on form.

The most common theme *description* (42%) refers to discourse whose purpose is to articulate what the artwork looks like and to understand its form. Depending on the artwork, different aspects come under consideration. In the conversation below, the texture, shape, and colour of the paintings are seen as salient, as well as their impact on each other.

S3	…the material reminds me of skin – it's soft
S2	the other one – is this was – it has an organic quality – I like the colours on the frame – and the way she's worked on it
T	I don't think I'm too keen on the oval shape
S3	it's more interesting – I don't know whether if there were more colour
T	it's going outside – it doesn't even have rectangles
S4	it has a tactile quality – it's very reminiscent of a biological quality – like an embryo – the frame painting lets it expand outside
S2	they do work well together – this one is more shiny – the other one is more subtle…

While description is intended to be an objective form of analysis, we can see from the extract how easily it can shade into a more subjective form of appreciation.

Students S3's "it's soft" is clearly approving, as is S2's "it has an organic quality" followed by "I like the colours". Although the tutor can call students out on such subjectivity, on this occasion she is complicit: "I don't think I'm too keen on the oval shape".

Throughout the texts there are a number of examples of subjective judgements about formal characteristics from both tutor and students. Powerful as they are, these are ultimately aesthetic judgements which are notoriously hard to explain and about which there may not be consensus.

The second largest theme *analysis* (41%) considers the question, "why this form and not another?" So for example the first question for one presenter about the pictures in his presentation is "some are images and some are painted – is there a reason?"; a student observing that "the installation here is pre-recorded" wants to know "is that intentional?"; the tutor asks one student "you mentioned your choice of images and structure – how do you make a formal decision about what you select – how do you make your choice?"; or asks another, "what was the reason for dressing the doll like that?"

If as we have seen above description can lead to subjective responses, analysis tends to be more objective, not "do I like it?" but "is it successful?"

Analysis links to intention, since perceptions of the appropriateness of the form will depend on perceptions of what the artwork is saying. Aspects of form may not always fit with what we know of the artwork's intentions however. For example, when discussing a feminist women-in-business installation, a student sees the fact that its messages are sewn as inappropriate since sewing is part of the a female stereotype:

S1　the type is confusing – it would be more appropriate if it was newspaper print – it's lovingly sewn – more sentimental

---

The tutor's response, however, reconciles the sewing with the installation's intention by seeing a more complex relationship between them:

T… yes about the type face – but it's also an investment of time that says I need to invest that time…

As she observes elsewhere:

T　…there are serious issues dealt with by sewing

11: THEMATIC ANALYSIS FINDINGS 153

Similarly, for a project in which involves notes written to each other by two art students who never meet, the tutor suggests that an email exchange would be more realistic, and therefore more appropriate, than hand-written notes. The visiting tutor however reconciles the form of the notes with their intention by developing a more subtle interpretation of what the artwork is saying:

T1 …there's an intimacy you've implied by it's being hand-written – you're not copying an e-mail – you're not e-mailing each other even though one would be forgiven for thinking OK why not why aren't they emailing each other – so there's something that is both public and private

If the analysis of form can uncover or modify intentions, it can also subvert them. A good example is an installation whose form initially inspires serious analysis:

S1 it's got a sort of real quality about it which is not a bad thing but when I looked at it I thought it was linked to organic structures like cells and neurons and stuff

Until the tutor confesses it reminds her of Christmas decorations:

T   you know what I mean – I think sometimes you know it's the time – they're balls – we could stick them on our tree you know

Interestingly, analysis often involves using similes and metaphor to make the connection between the visual form and what it represents. An abstract painting is "very reminiscent of a biological quality – like an embryo"; an installation "could be a cathedral" or "old-fashioned tupperware – you know it's like a mottled creamy colour"; in a mobile installation, "the space is like a baby's crib and…they're all like rounded planets…".

The final theme is around *variation* (17%) where students are encouraged to experiment with different forms. For the tutor, using varied forms is about finding different ways of saying the same thing. Responding to a video presentation involving a range of styles, she observes that "it definitely changes but there's an underlying style – the materiality brings it all together". For the students, the pressure to experiment can be quite challenging, for example for the students who confesses, "I hate performance".

11.2.12 Documentation (D)

The final theme, documentation, is a mandatory part of the assessment process for the students' artwork. Important as it is, the percentage of discourse relating to documentation in the sample is generally very low.

This changes with the arrival of the visiting tutor however (Text H). Faced with a succession of unfamiliar artworks, the tutor compares himself to a visitor to an art gallery who's dependent on the documentation for quick insights into what he's seeing. So he puts the emphasis on easy access where, for example, bullet points need to be standalone and not part of a narrative so that they can be skimmed strategically. The visiting tutor is aware of the tension between the students' remit to explain their work thoroughly and his own requirement for rapid access. His suggestion is to produce a short guide followed by a longer account consisting of a "more in depth detailed and maybe narrativised account of how you got to where you are in doing the work." Segmenting the documentation in this way will meet both the students' and the viewers' requirements.

Another concern of the visiting tutor is with the congruence between the documentation and the artwork. The tutor needs to be able to trust that the information in the documentation will lead to the "right" reading of the artwork. Incongruities occur when something is missing from the documentation, when the style of the documentation leads to expectations which are then not fulfilled by the artwork; when the content of the documentation is so overwhelming that's hard to see what the work might be; or when the documentation doesn't do justice to the artwork.

In the literature of art as a discipline, there is often uneasiness about the requirement for documentation insofar as it represents the university's preference for "conceptualising the product of the experience" rather than trying to understand the "experience of making" (Elkins, 2006, p. 246). Certainly relying on the students' documentation for access to their artworks seems altogether different from the quasi-mystical possibilities of experiencing an artwork described by Davey:

> In reflective consciousness, we learn that things are always more than they appear in any one instance...it is in this participatory space that an artwork can commence its endless work of unfolding its inexhaustible subject matter. (Davey, 2006, p. 33)

Documentation seems primarily pragmatic, a kind of quick-start guide for examiners short of time.

11.3 The distribution of the themes

Of all these themes, the question now is which are the most important? Figure 12 below shows how much of the discourse is allocated to each of the themes, calculated as percentages of the total.

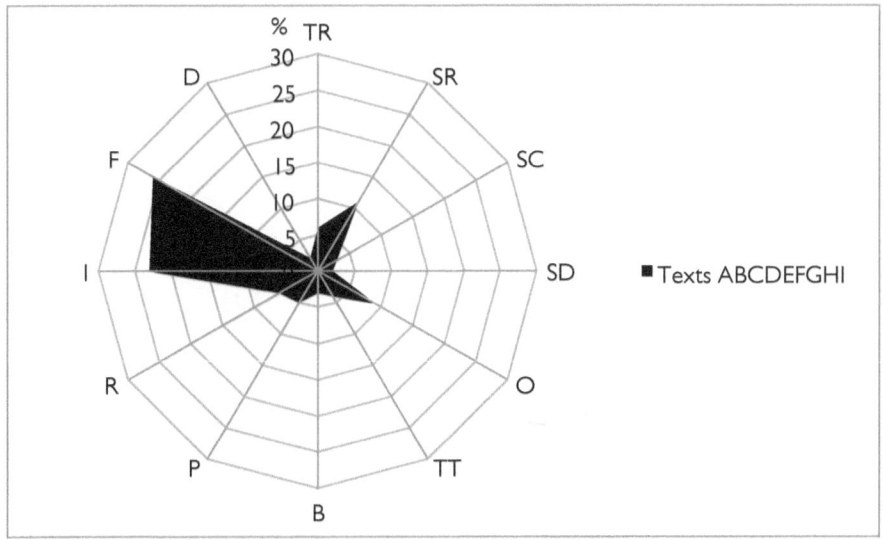

Figure 12. The distribution of the themes.

In theory we can only draw very cautious conclusions from this analysis, since clearly it isn't generalizable: different events with different tutors and students in different institutions would give different patterns. But in fact the pattern here is so strong as to make these concerns moot. According to the analysis, just two themes are responsible for almost half the studio discourse (49%): intention and form. The remaining themes are minor by comparison (Tutor's role and responsibilities = 6%; Students' role and responsibilities = 11%; Studio culture = 3%; Studio discourse = 2%; Operational concerns = 9%; Tools and techniques = 4%; Project brief = 3%; Professional practice = 5%; Research = 6%; Documentation = 2%.)

If we look more closely at the relationship between form and intention, we can see that individual artworks can be critiqued in terms of either form or intention or both, depending on the nature of the artwork. For example in the exchange below, the tutor (T) and the visiting tutor (T1) agree that the artwork they are looking at, a large-scale installation featuring melted materials, is about the exploration of form: there's no point in pursuing ulterior meanings.

T	…it's interesting that T1 has purely described it in formal terms as well which indicates a kind of honesty that it is about the materials – not about either an emotional or you know philosophical or whatever – we're not going there
T1	I think if part of your intention is that it should be any way be political I don't feel it at all

In another artwork made up of felt blocks, however, its intention – or lack of it – is the issue.

S2	I thought there might be writing on them to explain
S3	it's a failure – we didn't find the intention
S1	the intention is to look at them – to see and touch them – should they be displayed with writing
S3	maybe they're designed for something else – a game
S4	no – they would fit in a child's room but the signs say they're more like toys
S5	they could be for a game like building blocks but that won't work…

Other discussions move seamlessly between intention and form, as in the extract below.

S	it's too poppy – not tacky enough – I thought I'd put it all together into an installation – the idea would be walking through someone's head – memories – using general images – for the future I want to experiment with creating different images from the internet and old photos – I want to use time-based media to explore memory
S2	some are images and some are painted – is there a reason
S	it's organic – as you work it changes and becomes more of yourself
S3	why have you diversified like this
S1	don't know – it's better than before I think
S3	why
S	these are deep questions

Here the student's initial comments about his film on the nature of memory are about intention: "the idea would be walking through someone's head – memories", followed by formal concerns: "I want to use time-based media to explore memory". The first student question is about form: "some are images and some

11: THEMATIC ANALYSIS FINDINGS

are painted – is there a reason", while the second is about intention: "it's organic – as you work it changes and becomes more of yourself" in a way which determines much of the remainder of the crit, leading the presenting student to reflect that "these are deep questions".

The tutor's conclusion of a mainly formal crit of a student film with the comment "if we had time we'd go into your intention – what it's about" suggests that both intention and form would ideally be given equal time, but that this isn't always possible. This is the problem noted by Elkins (2001) when he reflects that:

> …the average critique is too short to really get at the work…it takes five or ten minutes just to see the work…in the next twenty minutes the teacher acclimates herself to the work…the really interesting, difficult questions are only just ready to be asked when a half-hour critique is drawing to a close. (Elkins, 2001, p. 119)

Figure 13 below provide a more detailed analysis of the distribution of intention and form in the critiques of the 17 individual artworks discussed in Text F.

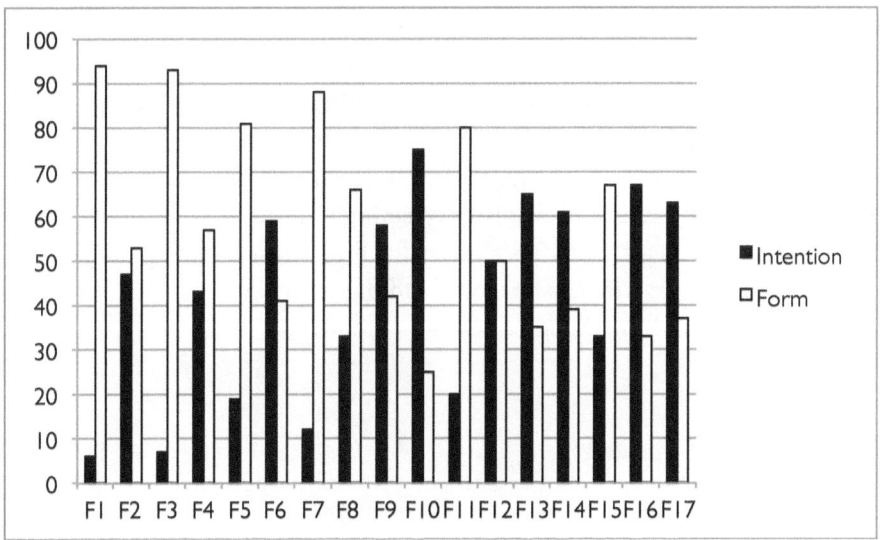

Figure 13. Themes of *Intention* and *Form* by crit in Text F.

Here, three of the crits achieve a balance between intention and form (F2, F4, & F12), seven focus more on intention (F6, F9, F10, F13, F14, F16, & F17), while the remaining seven focus more on form (F1, F3, F5, F7, F8, F11, & F15). We can see that the crits focusing on form are less likely to also include intention.

Given the high number of artworks involved, it may be that time pressure leads to less speculative critiques.

Clearly the themes of form and intention are intrinsically related, with the physical form of the artwork embodying abstract intentions. As we have seen above, this can lead to rapid concrete-abstract transitions. It can also lead to the paradox that crits can be at once explorations of "inaccessible, unlit, dangerous, and utterly seductive" ideas and at the same time "more limited and conventional than we might wish" (Elkins, 2001, pp. 191, 176). What they have in common however is an interest in creation of meaning.

11.4 Thematic analysis and the Framework of Educational Assumptions

Mapping the themes of the discourse to the Framework of Educational Assumptions is no easy task, given the tendency for each theme to turn up in more than one quadrant. For example the theme of the Students' role and responsibilities (SR) maps to the Normal Science quadrant in that students attend the tutor's sessions, work hard, and conform to the university's requirements, and also to the Professional Practice quadrant where they learn the tools and techniques of the trade. But the theme also maps to Extraordinary Science which requires intellectual and imaginative autonomy, and to Voodoo where the students' ideas may originate. This is the problem of stretch noted by Elkins (2006), whereby Fine Art invariably stretches the normal meaning of terms to their limits, to the extent that he argues for a new vocabulary for Fine Art use only (p. 243).

Judgments can nevertheless be made, and Figure 15 below shows a rich picture representation of the themes in each quadrant.

11: THEMATIC ANALYSIS FINDINGS

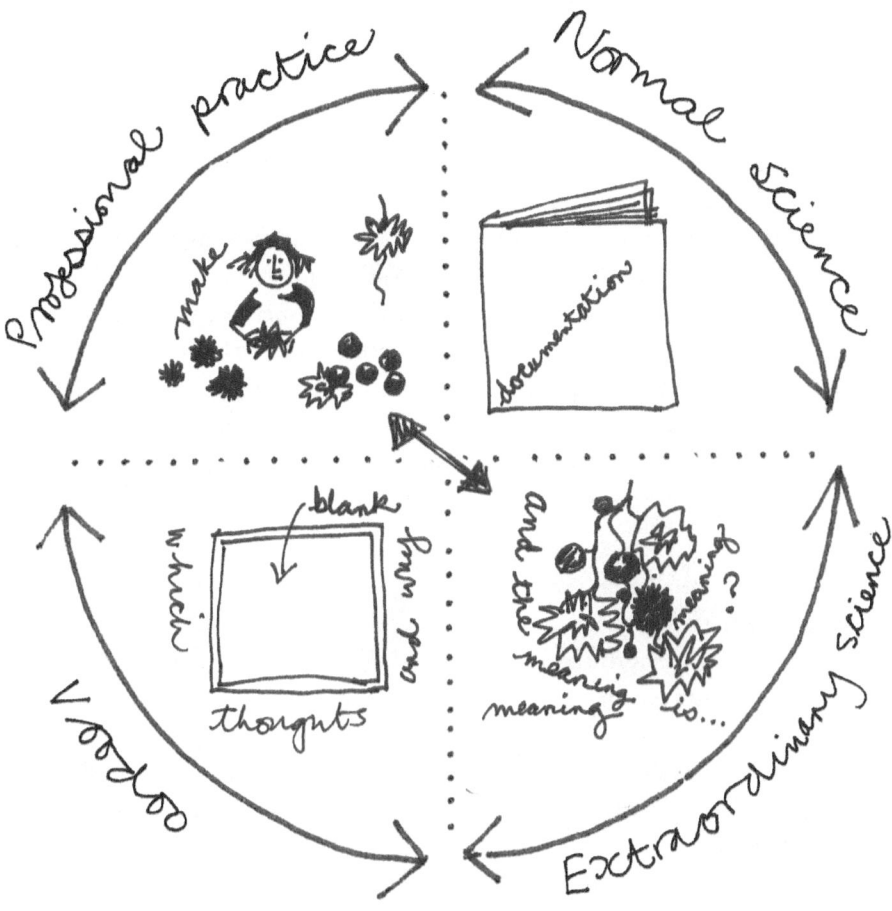

Figure 15. A rich picture representation of the relationship between the thematic analysis and the Framework of Educational Assumptions.

11.4.1 Normal Science

The Normal Science quadrant is represented by an image of the documentation students need to produce for their degree. Although the students have some say in terms of its form and content, it also has to conform to university standards of completeness, literacy, organisation and access.

Also included in this quadrant are research into other artists and the role of the tutor as an authority figure who monitors the students' behaviour and progress. Organisational activities such as devising timetables, planning work, working hard and complying with course deadlines and requirements also belong here.

11.4.2 Professional Practice

The Professional Practice quadrant is represented by the image of the student producing the "stuff" so valued by the tutor.

Other themes relating to this quadrant include the tools and techniques associated with the development of technical skills and tacit knowledge (Polanyi, [1958]1973), and also the ability to read the visual dimensions of colour, shape, texture, and space in a way which is a hallmark of the professional in all visual fields. Also included is the theme of the professional art world and discourse about how the students can best prepare for their professional careers. Finally, the project brief also belongs to this quadrant as an example of professional problem-solving in response to a task set by the tutor.

11.4.3 Extraordinary Science

The Extraordinary Science quadrant is represented by the image of the students' artwork at the centre of the search for meaning. This is the quadrant of autonomy, where students set their own briefs and decide how, when, and where they will carry out their work. The theme which is unique to Extraordinary Science, and which distinguishes it from the purely subjective Voodoo, is intention, the articulation of ideas and intuitions which at their best represent new ways of seeing the world.

In this quadrant the tutor's role shifts from the traditional authority figure to the supportive coach. The students' role correspondingly shifts from conformity to autonomy.

11.4.4 Voodoo

The Voodoo quadrant is represented by the image of the blank canvas asking Hanrahan's (2006) question "which thoughts and why".

The tutor makes no direct reference to this quadrant in the text. Indeed in one case she rejects an artwork because the student has chosen visual forms simply because she likes them. The tutor makes it clear that work based purely on personal feelings is not art although it may be craft, since the objects in themselves "pretty and well-made".

However references to the hidden world of feelings, beliefs, memories, and intuitions do occur as subthemes of form and intention in the student presentation texts, where the students have the opportunity to talk about their sources

11: THEMATIC ANALYSIS FINDINGS 161

of inspiration. For example, in the extract below the student whose work is based on myth clearly has a more than intellectual engagement with his subject matter:

S	with the mythology your work is based on – I'm interested in how you related to myth – how real it was to you…
P1	…a belief system not a religion with rules – I did have a deeper belief doing the research – we look outwards – transcendence – so it's more of a relocation – looking back into the human body – it's something I believed in- to look more internally – so it's played a big role in what I'm doing

Similarly the student exploring memory chooses to engage with her own memories for her experiments with form. Interestingly, the student herself is unhappy with this level of subjectivity and is anxious to find more "cognitive or conceptual" forms.

S3	are you going to explore the memories in your head or of someone famous
P1	I did mine – I don't like the idea of exploiting someone else's
S4	with the memories do you want to progress in other ways
P1	they're not fixed – they could become more realistic – I've thought about how memories don't exactly capture what happened
S4	they're mediated by film – have you thought about constructing the dream images yourself
P1	it's an interesting idea – I'm not happy with the installation – it's not thematic or conceptual enough – I'm into more cognitive stuff…

In another example, a student makes the connection between form and the unconscious through his interest in automatic drawing which he defines as "drawing without knowing you're drawing…I have control but they're also themes and issues from the subconscious".

For the tutor, drawing on personal beliefs or experiences in this way is allowable as long as the result is coherent: whether or not she believes in the mystical associations of automatic drawing, for example, she can see that "the actual images you come up with are very good".

Mapping the themes of studio discourse to the Framework of Educational Assumptions challenges the traditional dynamic where the Framework is divided in two. The thematic analysis shows that, in the discourse of Fine Art, all parts of the Framework are included, with an important dynamic between form in the Professional Practice segment and intention in Extraordinary Science. There is no separation between the top and bottom halves of the Framework and no corresponding distortion.

Accustomed as we are to the assumptions of the university disciplines which rely on separation and differentiation to define them, the fact that the discourse of Fine Art crosses these boundaries is a strong reason for the problem of explanation.

12: Art as Extraordinary Science

'20% of a degree course [should be] devised in free expression.'[53]

12.1 A 21st century paradigm

In Part 2 we saw how the historical narrative of Fine Art education seems to come to a stop after the Bauhaus, leaving art schools with versions of the modernist paradigm which have come to seem increasingly outdated in a world characterised by social, economic and technological change.

This lack of a contemporary paradigm is not for want of trying. For example the publisher's introduction to Madoff's *Art School: propositions for the 21st Century* (2009) describe how thirty of the art world's brightest and best educational thinkers have been brought together to come up with an answer to precisely this question.

> The last explosive change in art education came nearly a century ago, when the German Bauhaus was formed. Today, dramatic changes in the art world – its increasing professionalization, the pervasive power of the art market, and fundamental shifts in art-making itself in our post-Duchampian era – combined with a revolution in information technology, raise fundamental questions about the education of today's artists. *Art School (Propositions for the 21st Century)* brings together more than thirty leading international artists and art educators to reconsider the practices of art education in academic, practical, ethical, and philosophical terms…And throughout the volume, attention is paid to new initiatives and proposals about what an art school can and should be in the twenty-first century – and what it shouldn't be. No other book on the subject covers more of the questions concerning art education today or offers more insight into the pressures, challenges, risks, and opportunities for artists and art educators in the years ahead.[54]

Similarly 2006's Manifesta 6 conference publishes the reflections of nine internationally recognized artists and educationalists in its *Notes for an Art School*, while 2014's conference *Deschooling Society* brings radical sociological perspectives into the mix.

---

53 D.K. & V. H., 1969, p. 86

54 Retrieved 25 September 2015 from https://mitpress.mit.edu/books/art-school

Deschooling Society takes its title from Ivan Illich's seminal 1971 book, one of the most influential radical critiques of the education system in Western countries. Issues at the heart of that critique have been increasingly debated within the art world in recent years, and the subject of education has attracted renewed attention from artists, curators and collectives. Pedagogical models are currently being explored, re-imagined and deployed by practitioners from around the world in highly diverse projects comprising laboratories, discursive platforms, temporary schools, participatory workshops and libraries.[55]

Yet for all that the long-awaited 21st Century paradigm is as elusive as ever. It seems that in failing to explain itself to the university, art education has also failed to find its own explanation. And by the same logic, if the Framework of Educational Assumptions provides us with a way of explaining art education to the university, it also provides art itself with a new paradigm: that of Extraordinary Science.

The evidence for art as Extraordinary Science comes from the discourse analysis research described in the previous chapters. We have said that the generalisability of the research is limited, since the texts are specific to a particular time and place, and could be different with a different sample of texts, different tutors and students, or a different university. For example, the relatively low proportion of discourse relating to personal emotions and intuitions (Voodoo) observed here might be greater somewhere else, or with a tutor with different interests.[56]

And yet it spite of these reservations, the association of contemporary art education with Extraordinary Science emerges with startling clarity. The structural analysis shows how Fine Art educational discourse has little in common with the traditional teaching structures typical of the Normal Science or Professional Practice quadrants, which are dominated by the authority of the teacher. Art students are not in the business of doing what's already been done, however well they might be able to do it. And if art education is not primarily Normal Science or Professional Practice, it's clearly not Voodoo either, the realm of the purely subjective.

Art students are in the business of articulating their new versions of the world until such time as, with any luck, their ideas become accepted as the new Normal Science. They are extraordinary scientists.

- - - - -

55 Retrieved January 12, 2014, from www.southbankcentre.co.uk/find/hayward-gallery-and-visual-arts/visual-arts-talks-and-events/tickets/deschooling-society-52395

56 Elkins (2001) for example sees critiques as "like seductions, full of emotional outbursts" (p. 132), with examiners "daydreaming or fee-associating" (p. 131) as they make their comments, suggesting a more subjective style than that observed in this research.

12.2 Teaching Extraordinary Science

We've seen that the paradigm of Extraordinary Science is problematic for universities because although it's highly valued in theory, in practice it's not taught. As Thomas Kuhn ([1962]1970) unpicks the history of science, it becomes increasingly clear to him that the seismic paradigm shifts of Extraordinary Science are not taught in any normal university classroom:

> No part of the aim of Normal Science is to call forth new sorts of phenomena: indeed those that will not fit the box are often not seen at all…Normal Science does not aim at novelties of fact or theory and, when successful, finds none. (Kuhn 1970, pp. 24, 52)

Indeed Kuhn's worry about the inability of universities to produce the paradigms of the future has become a reality. Notoriously in the world of technology, we have seen how Stanford Ovshinsky changes the Japanese economy by inventing flat-screen technology without either attending or being recognised by the university system (Brooks, 2011, 205-210), while Steve Jobs, Bill Gates, and Mark Zuckerberg make their fortunes and change the world by dropping out of the university system. Indeed this is now something of a cliché, as evidenced by the National Enquirer's headline *Most billionaires don't have a college degree!*

> Wanna be a billionaire? Then drop out of college. Shockingly that's what the world's wealthiest folks – like Microsoft's Bill Gates and Facebook's Mark Zuckerberg – did. Amazingly, Gates, the world's richest man with $79 billion, and Zuckerberg, with $35 billion are Harvard University dropouts. And a study of the 100 richest people found that a staggering 32 had no college degree at all! (National Enquirer, 2015)

Yet in terms of science teaching, not much seems to have changed as a result. According to Brooks (2011), science students continue to be forced through an exhaustive curriculum characterised by experiments which rarely work as they are supposed to: science is seen as "dull, spiritless and cautious" (p. 255), and a career in science a "dull, dismal road less travelled" (p. 256). Only the most resilient and unimaginative students are likely to survive (p. 256), and there is a general "disengagement from science through tedium" (p. 259).

Even Kuhn (1970), who is clear that science education is lacking in some important dimension, has no idea of how to fix it (or if it is fixable):

> "How an individual invents (or finds he has invented) a new way of giving order to data now all assembled – must here remain inscrutable and may be permanently so." (Kuhn, 1970, p. 90)

But if art students are indeed extraordinary scientists, then it follows that art may have a very particular contribution to make to the problem of developing extraordinary scientists within the university system.

What would teaching Extraordinary Science to scientists look like? Let's imagine.

In terms of the science curriculum, we can start with the Hornsey students' argument that if art students need to spend 20% of the curriculum on academic study in the interests of balance, then science students should spend the same amount of time in "free expression" (D.K. & V. H., 1969, p. 86). So our imaginary Extraordinary Science module is mandatory and occupies a day a week.

Let's imagine Day 1 in the Extraordinary Science space. Just as the art tutor had some explaining to do, so the science tutor will take some time to explain the premise of the Extraordinary Science module. No-one will tell the students what to do – they're expected to come up with their own ideas (based, Kuhn suggests, on their individual awareness of anomalies) and plan their own investigations, manage their own time and learn to use tools and techniques as their investigation requires them.

Let's imagine that the tutor spends her time talking through her students' progress with them individually. Every few weeks everyone will come together for a crit where each student takes it in turn to have the floor, displaying their work and answering questions from tutors and peers. At the end of term, students can summarise their progress in presentations to their peers, followed by questions and suggestions.

Throughout these activities, the tutor will responsible for ensuring that the discourse stays open to the students' ideas and opinions rather than imposing her own superior knowledge.

At the end of the year, assessments will be carried out in the traditional way. Some ideas will have worked well, others less so. Some students will have played it safe, while others may have taken one risk too many. But for Brooks (2011), this experience of risk-taking is the necessary antidote to the myth of the scientist "taught to play to a set of rules" and to follow "a safe, efficient, controllable Method"(p. 5). Extraordinary scientists need to have the confidence to follow their hunches, argue their case and accept their failures, just as artists do.

12.3 Case study: Steve Jobs

As good way to end as any is with Isaacson's (2011) biography of Steve Jobs, whose ability to change a paradigm in any given field is by any measure extraordinary.

12: ART AS EXTRAORDINARY SCIENCE

…he launched a series of products over three decades that transformed whole industries:

- The Apple II, which took Wozniak's circuit board and turned it into the first personal computer that was not just for hobbyists.
- The Macintosh, which begat the home computer revolution and popularized graphical user interfaces.
- Toy Story and other Pixar blockbusters which opened up the miracle of digital imagination.
- Apple stores, which reinvented the role of a store in defining a brand.
- The iPod, which changed the way we consume music.
- The iTunes store, which saved the music industry.
- The iPhone, which turned mobile phones into music, photography, video, email, and web devices.
- The App store, which spawned a new content-creation industry.
- The iPad, which launched tablet computing and offered a platform for digital newspapers, magazines, books, and videos.
- iCloud, which demoted the computer from its central role in managing our content and let all of our devices sync seamlessly.
- And Apple itself, which Jobs considered his greatest creation, a place where imagination was nurtured, applied, and executed in ways so creative that it became the most valuable company on earth.

(Isaacson, 2011, p. 566)

For Jobs, this ability to re-imagine and reinvent makes him an artist working with the medium of technology: Isaacson (2011) tells the story of how he has the signatures of the Macintosh team carved inside the launch machines because "real artists sign their work" (p. 134).

Two questions are particularly interesting to us here. The first is about the educational profile of Steve Jobs himself, and how he became an extraordinary scientist. The second is about his role in building Apple as a company focussed on developing other extraordinary scientists.

Isaacson's account of Steve Jobs' early education is not simply that of a brilliant child bored and frustrated by the slow pace of school. There are certainly elements of that, as when his parents are advised to move him up two grades. His real issue, however, is with the nature of intellectual authority. Talking of his first experience of school, he reflects that:

I encountered authority of a different kind than I had ever encountered before, and I did not like it. And they really almost got me. They came close to really beating any curiosity out of me. (Isaacson, 2011, p.12)

His only salvation is a teacher who's prepared to go off the grid, giving him a hobby kit for grinding a lens and making a camera (p. 13) to keep his curiosity alive.

In many ways we can read all of Steve Jobs' subsequent intellectual history in terms of this early and instinctive resistance to the limits imposed by traditional paradigms. In high school, for example, he rejects the arts/science distinction. He may well be an electronics geek, but he is also equally engaged with music, literature and creative endeavours (p. 19). He remembers his English teacher as inspirational, but lasts only one year in the electronics class which he finds frustrating.

Famously, Jobs doesn't apply to Stanford university, on the grounds that:

> the kids who went to Stanford, they already knew what they wanted to do…they weren't really artistic. I wanted to do something that was more artistic and interesting. (Isaacson, 2011, p.33)

Instead he chooses Reed College, a liberal arts college in Portland, Oregon famous for the "free-spirited, hippie lifestyle" (p.33) of its students. There Jobs discovers Buddhism, meditation and psychedelic drugs, along with the realisation that:

> … an intuitive understanding and consciousness was more significant than abstract thinking and intellectual analysis. (Isaacson, 2011, p.35)

Yet even Reed's curriculum proves too restrictive. Jobs only wants to attend classes that interest him such as for example dance and calligraphy (p. 40). In a way which resonates with the Hornsey students' paradigm of the network or geodesic dome he officially drops out of college but continues to audit interesting classes for a further 18 months.

In terms of our Framework of Educational Assumptions, we can see how Issaacson's (2011) description of Jobs' daily routine in his early twenties includes all the quadrants:

> He meditated in the mornings, audited physics classes at Stanford, worked nights at Atari, and dreamed of starting his own business. (Isaacson, 2011, p.57)

The day starts in the Voodoo quadrant with meditation, moves to Normal Science in the afternoons with classes at Stanford, and turns to Professional Practice with working nights at Atari, all the while infused with dreams of changing the world in Extraordinary Science.

Jobs' challenge in building Apple is to manage the organisational paradox like every art school leader before him. And not unlike Gropius, his management style is often associated with legendary levels of dysfunction. According to one ex-employee:

> In my 3 years at Apple I've never observed so much confusion, fear and dysfunction... we are perceived by the rank and file as a boat without a rudder, drifting away into foggy oblivion. (Isaacson, 2011, p.197)

Ultimately, the paradox is resolved by the appointing the right people – "creative, wickedly smart and slightly rebellious" (p. 142) – and giving them free rein. There may be psychodramas along the way as particular ideas are criticised or rejected. There may even be "brilliant failures" like the NeXT computer cube (p. 219). But in the world of Extraordinary Science, all ideas are taken seriously for their potential to change the world.

> In so many other companies ideas and great design get lost in the process. The ideas that come from me and my team would have been completely irrelevant, nowhere, if Steve hadn't been there to push us, work with us, and drive through all the resistance to turn our ideas into practice. (Isaacson, 2011, p.347)

Steve Jobs' pitch to a programmer reluctant to join him reads as a call to extraordinary scientists everywhere, whatever their discipline.

> We are inventing the future. Think about surfing on the front edge of a wave. It's really exhilarating. Now think about dog-paddling at the tail end of that wave. It wouldn't be anywhere near as much fun. Come down here and make a dent in the universe. (Isaacson, 2011, p.96)

References

Abbott, A. D. (1988). *The system of professions.* University of Chicago Press.
Adams, D., Bos, S., & Haacke, H. (2009). Conversation. In S. H. Madoff (Ed.), *Art school: Propositions for the 21ˢᵗ century* (pp. 257-270). Cambridge, Massachusetts and London: The MIT Press.
Alexander, R. (Ed.) (2010). Children, their world, their education: Final report and recommendations of the Cambridge Primary Review. London and New York: Routledge.
Ashbee, C. R. (1911). *Should we stop teaching art?* London: B. T. Batsford.
Badiou, A. (2005). *Handbook of inaesthetics.* Stanford University Press.
Becker, H. S. (1990). Generalizing from case studies. In E. W. Eisner, & A. Peshkin (Eds.), *Qualitative inquiry in education* (pp. 233-242) . New York and London: Teachers College, Columbia University.
Bergdoll, B. & Dickerman, L. (2009). *Bauhaus 1919-1933: Workshops for modernity.* New York: The Museum of Modern Art.
Birnbaum, D. (2009). Teaching art: Adorno and the devil. In S. H. Madoff (Ed.), *Art school: Propositions for the 21ˢᵗ century* (pp. 231-246). Cambridge, Massachusetts and London: The MIT Press.
Black, M. (1973). Notes on design education in Great Britain. In D. W. Piper (Ed.), *After Hornsey: Readings in art and design education: 1* (pp. 29-45). London: Davis-Poynter.
Bowker, C. & Star, S. L. (2000). *Sorting things out: Classification and its consequences.* Cambridge, Massachusetts and London: The MIT Press.
Brighton, C. R. R. (1992). *Research in Fine Art: An epistemological and empirical study.* Unpublished doctoral dissertation, University of Surrey.
Brooks, M. (2011). *Free radicals: The secret anarchy of science.* London: Profile Books Ltd.
Bryman, A. ([2001]2008). *Social Research methods.* Oxford: Oxford University Press.
Burke Johnson, R. B. & Onwuegbuzie, A. J. (2004). Mixed methods research: a research paradigm whose time has come. *Educational Researcher, 33*(7), pp. 14-26.
Cameron, D. ([2001]2006). *Working with spoken discourse.* London, New Delhi and California: Sage Publications Inc.
Checkland, P. ([1984]1998). *Systems thinking, systems practice.* Chichester, New York, Brisbane and Toronto: John Wiley & Sons.

Checkland, P. & Scholes, J. ([1990]1993). *Soft systems methodology in action*. Chichester, New York, Brisbane and Toronto: John Wiley & Sons.

Cook-Sather, A. (2003). Movements of mind: The matrix, metaphors and re-imagining education. *Teachers College Record, 105*(6), 946-977.

Corning, P. A. (2002). The re-emergence of "emergence": A venerable concept in search of a theory. *Complexity, 7*(6), 18-30. Retrieved January 20, 2013, from www.complexsystems.org

Coulthard, M. ([1977]1985). *An introduction to discourse analysis*. London and New York: Longman.

Daichendt, G. J. (2010). *Artist Teacher: A philosophy for creating and teaching*. Bristol, UK and Chicago: Intellect.

Davey, N. (2006). Art and *theoria*. In K. Macleod, & L. Holdridge (Eds.), *Thinking through art: Reflections on art as research* (pp. 20-39). London and New York: Routledge.

Davis, W. (1985). The serpent and the rainbow: A Harvard scientist's astonishing journey into the secret societies of Haitian voodoo, zombis, and magic. New York: Simon and Schuster.

de Bono, E. (2009). Lateral thinking: A textbook of creativity. Penguin.

de Duve, T. (1994). When form has become attitude – and beyond. In N. de Ville & S. Foster (Eds.), *The artist and the academy* (pp. 23-40). John Hansard Gallery, University of Southampton.

Dewey, J. ([1916]2007). Democracy and education: An introduction to the philosophy of education. NuVision publications.

D. K. & V. H. (1969). The roots of the revolution. In Association of Hornsey College of Art (Ed.), *The Hornsey affair: Students and staff of the Hornsey College of Art* (pp. 61-101). Penguin Books.

Dodds, E. R. (1951). *The Greeks and the irrational*. Berkeley, Los Angeles, London: University of California Press.

D. P. (1969). What happened: The first four days. In Association of Hornsey College of Art (Ed.), *The Hornsey affair: Students and staff of the Hornsey College of Art* (pp. 29-57). Penguin Books.

Efland, A. D. (1990). *A history of art education*. Teacher's College Press.

ElDahab, M. A. (2006). Kitsch, destruction and education: An interview with Thomas Rehberger. In *Notes for an art school: Manifesta 6* (pp. 1-7). Retrieved January 20, 2014, from www.manifesta.org/manifesta-6/

ElDahab, M. A. (2006a). On how to fall with grace – or fall flat on your face. In *Notes for an art school: Manifesta 6* (pp. 1-6). Retrieved January 20, 2014, from www.manifesta.org/manifesta-6/

Elkins, J. (2001). *Why art cannot be taught: A handbook for art students.* Urbana and Chicago: University of Illinois Press.

Elkins, J. (2006). Afterword: On beyond research and new knowledge. In K. Macleod & L. Holdridge (Eds.), *Thinking through art: Reflections on art* as *research* (pp. 241-247). London and New York: Routledge.

Elkins, J. (2008). *Art education is radically undertheorized: An interview with Cornelia Sollfrank.* Retrieved January 10, 2013, from http://thing-hamburg.de/index.php?id=796

Esche, C. (1990). Include me out: Preparing artists to undo the art world. In aS. H. Madoff (Ed.), *Art school: Propositions for the 21st century* (pp. 101-113). Cambridge, Massachusetts and London: The MIT Press.

Feinberg, W. (1983). *Understanding Education: Toward a reconstruction of educational enquiry.* Cambridge, London, New York, New Rochelle, Melbourne and Sydney: Cambridge University Press.

Feyerabend, P. (1975). *Against method.* London: Verso.

Foucault, M. ([1966] 2012). *The order of things: An archaeology of the human sciences.* London and New York: Routledge.

Foucault, M. ([1969]2002). *The archaeology of knowledge.* Routledge.

Garfinkel, H. (1967). *Studies in ethnomethodology.* Cambridge: Polity Press.

Goldstein, C. (1996). Teaching art: Academies and schools from Vasari to Albers. Cambridge University Press.

Hanrahan, S. (2006). Poesis. In K. Macleod, & L. Holdridge (Eds.), *Thinking through art: Reflections on art* as *research* (pp. 143-155). London and New York: Routledge.

Hochman, E. S. (1997). *Bauhaus: Crucible of modernism.* New York: Fromm International.

Hudson, L. ([1972]1974). *The cult of the fact.* London: Jonathan Cape.

Isaacson, W. (2011). *Steve Jobs.* London: Little, Brown.

Katz, V. (2003). Black Mountain College: Experimental in art. MIT Press.

Kestelman, M. (1973). The aim and content of art education. In D. W. Piper (Ed.), *After Coldstream: Readings in art and design education: 2* (pp. 46-54). London: Davis-Poynter.

Körner, S. (1974). *Categorial frameworks.* Oxford: Basil Blackwell.

Kuhn, T. S. ([1962]1970). *The structure of scientific revolutions.* Chicago and London: University of Chicago Press.

Lakoff, G., & Johnson, M. ([1980]2003). *Metaphors we live by.* Chicago and London: The University of Chicago Press.

Latour, B. ([2005]2007). Reassembling the social: An introduction to Actor-Network Theory. Oxford University Press.

Lloyd, G. E. R. (1966). *Polarity and analogy*. Cambridge, London, New York and Melbourne: Cambridge University Press.

Lowy, A. & Hood, P. ([2004]2010). The power of the 2 x 2 matrix: Using 2 x 2 thinking to solve business problems and make better decisions. Jossey-Bass.

Macdonald, S. (1973). Articidal tendencies: A history of the government's attitude to art and design education in England over the last hundred years. In D. W. Piper (Ed.), *After Coldstream: Readings in art and design education: 2* (pp. 89-99). London: Davis-Poynter.

Macleod, K., & Holdridge, L. (2006). Introduction. In K. Macleod, & L. Holdridge (Eds.), *Thinking through art: Reflections on art as research* (pp. 1-15). London and New York: Routledge.

Madge, C., & Weinberger, B. (1973). *Art students observed*. London: Faber and Faber.

McGilchrist, I. (2009). The master and his emissary: The divided brain and the making of the Western world. New Haven and London: Yale University Press.

"Michael Gove's history wars." (2013, March 1). The Times, p. 6.

Morris, H. (2011). I walked with a zombie: Travels among the undead. *Harper's Magazine, 323*, 52-61.

"Most billionaires don't have a college degree!" (2015, August 16). National Enquirer.

Ortony, A. ([1979]1998). Metaphor, language and thought. In A. Ortony, (Ed.), *Metaphor and thought* (pp. 1-18). Cambridge, New York and Melbourne: Cambridge University Press.

Peters, R. S. (1967). What is an educational process? In R. S. Peters (Ed.), *The concept of education* (pp. 1-23). London: Routledge & Kegan Paul.

Pevsner, N. (1940). *Academies of art past and present*. London, New York, Toronto, Bombay, Calcutta and Madrid: Cambridge University Press.

Philips, S. U. (1982). The language socialization of lawyers: Acquiring the "cant". In G. Spindler (Ed.), *Doing the ethnography of schooling: Educational anthropology in action* (pp. 176-209). New York, Chicago, San Francisco, Philadelphia, Montreal, Toronto, London, Sydney, Tokyo, Mexico City, Rio de Janeiro and Madrid: Holt, Rinehart and Winston.

Piper, D. W. (1973). Introduction and preface. In D. W. Piper (Ed.), *After Hornsey: Readings in art and design education: 1* (pp. 13-25). London: Davis-Poynter.

Polanyi, M. ([1958]1973). *Personal knowledge: Towards a post-critical theory*. London: Routledge and Kegan Paul.

Raqs Media Collective (2009). In In S. H. Madoff (Ed.), *Art school: Propositions for the 21st century* (pp. 71-81). Cambridge, Massachusetts and London: The MIT Press.
Read, H. (1953). *Education through art.* London: Faber and Faber.
Risenhoover, M. & Blackburn, R. T. (1976). *Artists as professors.* Urbana, Chicago and London: University of Illinois Press.
Rugoff, I. (2010, April). From discourse practices to the pedagogical turn. In R. Rugoff & S. Talent (Chairs). Discussion conducted at the conference *Deschooling Society,* London, England.
Schnapp, J. T. & Shanks, M. (2009). Atrereality (Rethinking craft in a knowledge economy). In S. H. Madoff (Ed.), *Art school: Propositions for the 21st century* (pp. 141-158). Cambridge, Massachusetts and London: The MIT Press.
Schön, D. ([1983]2007). *The reflective practitioner: How professionals think in action.* Ashgate Publishing Limited.
Schön, D. (1985). *The design studio: An exploration of its traditions and potentials.* London: ROBA Publications Ltd.
Schön, D. ([1993]1998). Generative metaphor: A perspective on problem-setting in social policy. In A. Ortony (Ed.), *Metaphor and thought* (pp. 137-163). Cambridge, New York and Melbourne: Cambridge University Press.
Stubbs, M. ([1983] 1995). *Discourse analysis: The sociolinguistic analysis of natural language.* Oxford: Basil Blackwell.
Thornton, S. ([2008]2009). *Seven days in the art world.* London: Granta.
Tickner, L. (2008). *Hornsey 1968: The art school revolution.* London: Francis Lincoln Limited.
T. N. (1969). Notes towards the definition of an anti-culture. In Association of Hornsey College of Art (Ed.), *The Hornsey affair: Students and staff of the Hornsey College of Art* (pp. 15-25). Penguin Books.
Waller, J. (2014) *A horse beside my writing desk: explaining fine art studio practice in the context of the university.* Unpublished doctoral dissertation, University of Reading.
Wenger, E. ([1998]2005). *Communities of practice: Learning, meaning and identity.* Cambridge, New York, Melbourne, Madrid, Cape Town, Singapore and São Paulo: Cambridge University Press.
Widdowson, H. G. ([2004]2007). *Text, context, pretext: Critical issues in discourse analysis.* UK (Oxford), and Australia: Blackwell Publishing.
Wilber, K. (1998). *The marriage of sense and soul.* New York: Broadway Books.

Woodham, J. & Lyon, P. (2009). Art and design at Brighton 1859-2009: From arts and manufacturers to the creative and cultural industries. Brighton: University of Brighton.

www.ingramcontent.com/pod-product-compliance
Lightning Source LLC
Chambersburg PA
CBHW031628210526
45464CB00004B/1800